WHAT ARE
THESE WOUNDS?

THE LIFE OF A CISTERCIAN MYSTIC

Saint Lutgarde of Aywières

By THOMAS MERTON

THE BRUCE PUBLISHING COMPANY
MILWAUKEE

Nihil obstat: Fr. M. Gabriel O'Connell, O.C.R.
Fr. M. Antonius Chassagne, O.C.R.
Imprimi potest: Fr. Dominicus Nogues, O.C.R., Abbas Generalis
Imprimatur: ✠ Joannes Alexander Floersh, D.D.,
Archiepiscopus Ludovicopolitanus
February 17, 1948

(Second Printing — 1950)

WHAT ARE THESE WOUNDS?

To The Cistercian Nuns
who are trying to love the
Sacred Heart of Jesus in
twentieth-century America
as He was once loved by
their great Patroness
St. Lutgarde of Aywières.

class as a stigma. This places her among the very earliest
Christian stigmatics. Yet although she stands on the threshold
of a spirituality that is distinctly "modern," St. Lutgarde's
mysticism springs from the purest Benedictine sources. Her
mystical contemplation, like that of St. Gertrude and St.
Mechtilde, is nourished almost entirely by the Liturgy. Above
all, it centers upon the Sacrifice of Calvary and upon the
Mass which continues that Sacrifice among us every day.

The charm of St. Lutgarde is heightened by a certain
earthy simplicity which has been preserved for us unspoiled
in the pages of her medieval biography. She was a great
penitent, but she was anything but a fragile wraith of a
person. Lutgarde, for all her ardent and ethereal mysticism,
remained always a living human being of flesh and bone.
When she was a young girl in the world she seems to have
been remarkably attractive, and we can imagine her as something more than merely pretty. She must have had one of
those marvelously proportioned Flemish faces, full of a
mature and serious beauty, which we find in the paintings
of the great Flemish masters of a later day than hers. She
must have looked like the "Virgins" of Van Eyck. In any
case, her entrance into the mystical life was not without an
element of excitement and romance. She was faced with no
mere abstract choice between heavenly and earthly love:
it was not the mere solution of a conflict of ideals which
brought her eventually to the cloister. She was carried into
the arms of Christ by circumstances that shook her to the
depths of her sensitive being.

The life of St. Lutgarde introduces us to a mysticism that
is definitely extraordinary. This is not the mysticism which
theologians claim to be a "normal" development of the
Christian life of grace and the infused virtues and the Gifts
of the Holy Ghost. Here we are in the presence of visions,
ecstasies, stigmata, prophecies, miracles. St. Lutgarde was a

PREFACE

IN THE month of June, when the sun burns high in the bright firmament and when Cistercian monks, like all other farmers, hitch up their teams and go out to gather in the wheat, St. Lutgarde's Day comes around in the Liturgical cycle. It is not a universal feast, celebrated by the whole Church. It belongs only to two Belgian dioceses and to the saint's own Order — the Cistercians. Yet she is a saint whose spirit is as ardent and colorful as the June weather and as bright as the tiger lilies that enliven the fields and roadsides of America in the month in which we celebrate her memory. And it is especially fitting that her feast should occur in the month of the Sacred Heart. St. Lutgarde was one of the great precursors of the devotion to the Sacred Heart of Jesus.

Seven hundred years ago, and some four hundred years before St. Margaret Mary labored and prayed and suffered for the institution of the Feast of the Sacred Heart, St. Lutgarde of Aywières had entered upon the mystical life with a vision of the pierced Heart of the Saviour, and had concluded her mystical espousals with the Incarnate Word by an exchange of hearts with Him. But there are other facts which make St. Lutgarde worthy of the attention of the theologian, the Church historian, and of all religious souls. She was a contemporary of St. Francis, the first recorded stigmatic, and she too had received a mystical wound in her heart which historians have not hesitated to "mystic" in the popular sense of that term, and her life was certainly colorful and extraordinary enough to make her popular with Catholics of our own time, too. Of course, medieval saints' lives abound in strange phenomena, and we are inclined to be a little suspicious of the facile enthusiasm with which so many pious writers of those days set down the deeds of their heroes as "miracles." But the biographer of St. Lutgarde, though occasionally suffering from the naïveté common in his age, is as reliable as anyone in the thirteenth century.

Thomas of Cantimpré, the author of the *Vita Lutgardis*[1] was a Dominican friar and a theologian of some ability. He had studied at Cologne, under St. Albert the Great, as a classmate of St. Thomas Aquinas. He had also studied at Paris gaining a Doctor's Degree in Theology. Afterward he taught theology and philosophy at Louvain. He was especially interested in mystical theology and in the direction of mystics. His writing springs from his practical experience and observation of souls in the great mystical ferment that swept the Low Countries in the thirteenth century. He wrote the life of Bl. Christine, "the admirable," whose levitations make her a worthy competitor for the honors of St. Joseph Cupertino, patron of airmen. He also wrote on Bl. Margaret of Ypres and Bl. Mary of Oignies, and capped it all with an allegory, the *Bonum Universale de Apibus,* in which he treats of moral and ascetic theology in a way that modern readers would find totally unpalatable.

His life of St. Lutgarde is a minor masterpiece. The Latin in which it is written is fresh and full of life and every page furnishes us with vivid little details that stamp his whole record of the saint's life with authenticity. Thomas of Cantimpré was writing an objective and lively story of the life of one he had known intimately for sixteen years. At the time

[1] *Acta Sanctorum Bollandiae*, June, ii, p. 187 ff.

when he wrote this biography, shortly after the saint's death,
Thomas of Cantimpré was prior of the Friars Preachers at
Louvain and shortly afterward he became suffragan bishop
of Cambrai. He took care to have all his statements carefully
checked, especially by another Dominican, Fra Bernard,
Penitentiary to Innocent II, who had also directed St. Lut-
garde. The authority of Thomas of Cantimpré is upheld by
Denis the Carthusian, St. Robert Bellarmine, and many others.

The *Vita Lutgardis* was popularized by the famous Carthusian Lawrence Surius in the fifteenth century. In the seventeenth century it was translated into Spanish and Italian.
There has never been an English translation of this life, nor
any full-length book on St. Lutgarde in our language. The
seventh centenary of the saint's death, in 1946, brought forth
several works in French and Flemish, but we did not have
access to these when the present volume was compiled. In any
case, Thomas of Cantimpré is the one authentic source for
all "lives" of St. Lutgarde. Many of the modern biographies
simply paraphrase Thomas, adding a veneer of pious reflec-
tions concerning the visions and miracles of the saint.

The present book was written before the *Seven Storey
Mountain*. It was undertaken as an anonymous pamphlet in
1945, at the Abbey of Gethsemani, at the earnest wish of the
Abbot of that Cistercian community, Dom M. Frederic
Dunne, of holy memory. Dom Frederic had great devotion
to St. Lutgarde, whom he resembled in his penitential
ardor and in his fervent devotion to the Sacred Heart of
Jesus. Her life expresses many of the themes that were
dearest to Dom Frederic's heart and which, indeed, must
always be dear to the heart of every contemplative monk:
the love of God, penance and reparation, intercession for
souls. But it cannot be too much stressed that in St. Lutgarde,
as in all the early Cistercians, the love that embraces penance
and hardship for the sake of Christ is never merely negative,

never descends to mere rigid formalism, never concentrates on mere exterior observance of fasts and other penitential rigors. The fire of love that consumed the heart of St. Lutgarde was something vital and positive and its flames burned not only to destroy but to rejuvenate and transform. It was this love that Christ came to cast upon the earth and which Dom Frederic did so much to enkindle in the Cistercian (Trappist) monasteries of America that came under his influence.

This book was written with no other purpose than to help American Catholics to love the Sacred Heart with something of that same purity, and simplicity, and ardor.[2]

[2] A pious pamphlet called "The Heavenly Court" has been circulated in the United States in recent years. It sets forth a devotion which is supposed to have been originated by "the Holy Cistercian nun St. Lutgarde of Brabant." The only Cistercian nun called St. Lutgarde is the subject of the present volume. Her monastery, Aywières, was indeed situated in Brabant. But there is no record of her having originated the devotion called "The Heavenly Court." No doubt there has been some mistake. The pamphlet called "The Heavenly Court" has nothing to do with St. Lutgarde of Aywières.

CONTENTS

xiii

CONTENTS

WHAT ARE THESE WOUNDS?

CHAPTER ONE

CHILDHOOD. STUDENT IN THE BENEDICTINE CONVENT. TWO SUITORS. HER FIRST MYSTICAL GRACES

BORN in 1182, Lutgarde reached maturity at the turn of the thirteenth century. She belongs to the age of St. Francis and St. Dominic, of St. Thomas Aquinas and St. Bonaventure, of Pope Innocent III and King St. Louis of France. It was an age that has been perhaps too much idealized, but it was nevertheless a great age. It saw the climax of many centuries of Christian culture and it witnessed a turning point in the social and religious history of the western world. Feudalism was coming to an end, a powerful commercial class was beginning to play a dominant part in civil life, especially in the great free cities of western Europe. A gradual but fundamental economic revolution was taking place, with profound effects on the whole structure of society, and the spiritual life of the Catholic Church was bound to be affected by it.

The thirteenth century was an age of conflict and contradiction. It was a century of great saints and great sinners, great greed and great charity, great mercy and great cruelty. The schoolmen were contemplating the deepest truths of theology and philosophy with a limpid serenity of vision that has never been equaled: but already, around them, less capable and less spiritual minds were preparing the decline of Christian thought by a sterile intellectualism without spirit and without insight. There were already powerful heresies abroad, heresies which affected thousands with unrest. Above all the new spirit of individualism that was born and developed with the commercial culture of the bourgeois class seemed to demand a special kind of spirituality of its own. With the growth of the new social Order, came the development of a new spirit in Christian devotion and Christian living. Collective, liturgical prayer ceased to have the influence it had exercised in the ages of St. Augustine and St. Benedict.

The liturgy ceased to be practically everything in Christian spirituality. Spirituality became more imaginative, affective, individual. It was a good and necessary development, as long as it did not degenerate into eccentricity. It was good for Christians to realize how intimate and personal a part the love of the crucified Redeemer was really meant to play in their individual lives. The sacred humanity of Jesus became a reality to which the saints of the thirteenth century were passionately, romantically, almost extravagantly devoted: but can there be extravagance in the love of God? St. Francis of Assisi trod the white roads of Umbria and Tuscany, singing his love of Christ in the tongue of the French troubadours, and everywhere the Franciscan and Dominican saints filled Europe with their ardent love of the crucified Saviour. As if to set the seal upon this new growth in spirituality, God Himself miraculously imprinted the wounds of Christ's Passion upon the flesh of Francis of Assisi. It was a vivid and direct and miraculous illustration of the truth that the highest perfection of the Christian life is union with the Son of God by a charity that extends to the limit of compassion, and which identifies the heart of the saint with the pierced Heart of Jesus crucified.

The child who received the name of Lutgarde in baptism in the ancient font of one of the churches of the Flemish city of Tongres in 1182 was to have an important part in all this. She was not called to found a new religious Order or to exercise the universal influence of St. Francis or St. Dominic or St. Catherine of Siena. Nevertheless, this future daughter of Bernard of Clairvaux was to make a significant contribution to the new development of Christian mysticism.

It was fitting that the Cistercians should play an important part in this new growth, for Bernard of Clairvaux had done more than any other individual to set the movement going. The sermons he preached on the *Canticle of Canticles*, in the Chapter House of his Abbey, to his community of White Monks, in the first half of the twelfth century, represented the final maturing of the mysticism of the Fathers and prepared the way for the ardent, lyrical devotion to Christ that would characterize the thirteenth-century Franciscans. But the Cistercians themselves were not to be excluded from the great new ferment of mysticism that dominated the thirteenth century. Indeed the Cistercians were to have a place of honor as the leading mystics of the Low Countries in that age of visions and stigmatization.

The names of the contemplatives who flourished in Cistercian monasteries and convents in Brabant and Flanders and in the Rhineland and Saxony between twelve hundred and the end of the fourteenth century are not perhaps as famous as they ought to be. Only St. Gertrude has won a place on the calendar of the universal Church. St. Mechtilde is fairly well known, Bl. Mechtilde of Magdeburg also. The Belgian mystics of the Order of Citeaux are still invoked and commemorated in their own land. St. Lutgarde is one of the patrons of Belgium, and so is Bl. Ida of Louvain. There were two other Cistercian Idas – one of Nivelle and one of Leeuwen, who are remembered as great mystics. Bl. Beatrice of Nazareth also holds an important place among them. The Cistercian monks of the time furnish names that have been less well remembered — Bl. Arnulph the lay brother of Villers-en-Brabant, whose adventures read like pages from the *Fioretti*, is the only remarkable one among them.

Lutgarde, was born of a bourgeois father who, like the father of St. Francis, the merchant Pietro Bernardone of Assisi, cherished worldly ambitions for his children. Lutgarde's mother, a noblewoman, was capable of understanding a more spiritual ideal.

Early in Lutgarde's childhood the father arranged a profitable marriage. The affair involved, among other things, a commercial investment. He put his daughter's dowry money in the business of some merchant: but a cargo was lost at sea and the dowry went down with it. Lutgarde's family was not extremely wealthy and the marriage depended on money. The mother had a separate patrimony of her own, but when she was called upon to furnish a dowry she refused, saying that if she had to put up money at all she would only do so in order to get Lutgarde into a convent.

She bluntly told the little girl that if she wanted to become the spouse of Christ, she might indeed have a dowry. Otherwise, she would have to "marry a cowherd."

The little girl was not so young as to be unable to take an active interest in what was going on. She was nearing the age of twelve, and was not considered too young for marriage according to the standards of those times. She was pretty, and she evidently knew it. She had a taste for clothes that showed off her beauty to great advantage. She was fond of all the pleasures of friendship, without being frivolous or light-minded. The reason why her mother favored a convent for Lutgarde was that there were also deep seeds of spirituality beginning to germinate in the child's pure soul. Thomas of Cantimpré assures us that she already had something of that experimental sense of the presence of God dwelling within her which is one of the tokens of mystical prayer.

In any case, the mother had her way, and Lutgarde went off to the Benedictine convent of St. Catherine's, at St. Trond. It was a little outside the walls of the town, where the railway station stands today.

It is not quite clear whether Lutgarde entered the novitiate, or took up residence in the convent as a student or oblate. In view of what is to follow in her story, modern biographers of the saint tend to take it for granted that she was only a student.

Thomas of Cantimpré speaks of her entrance into the convent in terms that would seem to indicate at least the intention to became a nun. *Inter moniales ordinis S. Benedicti divino servitio mancipatur.* Indeed, the last three words: "she devoted herself to the service of God" seem to imply much more than that, since the verb *mancipari* has the meaning of being bound by strict obligation or even proprietorship and slavery to a master.[1] It is clear, however, that she had not made profession, although *mancipatur* would give us every right to suppose so. The actual account of her profession comes later in the narrative, as we shall see.[2]

On the other hand, it is difficult to see any basis for P. Jonquet's statement that she made application for the habit of novice in 1200, namely, after the somewhat dangerous adventures we are about to relate. All that can be said is that the position of novices in Benedictine convents at that time was not too well defined or regulated. It is hard to say if there was any general rule as to the length and conditions of noviceship, or indeed, if there was such a thing as the habit of novice. Let us say Lutgarde was some sort of postulant, not in the sense that she was subjected to any definite trial, but only that she was boarding in the convent, perhaps receiving

---

[1] *Vita, vol. cit,* 191 f. Cf. Forcellini, *Lexicon,* verbo "mancipo," and Ducange, *Glossarium, ibid.*

[2] *Vita,* I, xx, ii, 17, 194 c.

a little education and following the community exercises, with a more or less vague intention of becoming a nun in the course of time.

Two things are quite clear: she had definitely given herself, in some measure, to the convent life, but she had also retained her liberty to return to the world.

While she was in this condition, a young man fell in love with her and paid her frequent visits at the convent. Lutgarde, it appears, had no real intention of encouraging him: but her long intervals spent in worldly and perhaps guardedly sentimental conversations in the parlor were not discountenanced by the nuns, and were imitated by many other persons in the convent. This state of laxity so emboldened the young man that he once even entertained a criminal project of breaking into the house where Lutgarde had her dwelling, but he took fright and gave up his designs.

Lutgarde, still very young, seems to have been completely ignorant of the turn things were taking. Pleased and a little flattered by these attentions, she was content to have them continue. The mere fact that there was apparently "nothing wrong" in them was enough to set her uninstructed conscience at rest, until Christ Himself intervened, and made one of these meetings the occasion of His first great mystical grace to His future saint.

One day, while the simple girl was sitting behind the grille in the parlor listening to the whisperings of her admirer, Christ in His humanity suddenly appeared, blazing before her astonished eyes. He revealed the spear-wound in His side, and said to her: "Seek no more the pleasure of this unbecoming affection: behold, here, forever, what you should love, and how you should love: here in this wound I promise you the most pure of delights."

Lutgarde was struck with terror and love. Her eyes fixed themselves upon the wound in the Heart of Christ, she lost all consciousness of her surroundings and the sudden pallor of her face indicated to her visitor that something extraordinary had happened. Indeed, Lutgarde, penetrated to the depths of her soul by supernatural light, felt the shadows and darkness of her worldly affection completely dispelled, and forever.

Thomas of Cantimpré does not go into any detail in describing her emotions on recovering her senses. He simply tells us that she turned to her friend with the words: "Get away from me, thou bait of death, thou food of crime: I belong to another Lover."[3]

Nevertheless, if Lutgarde had now resolved to end all compromise with the duties of her state, the relaxed state of her convent did not afford her sufficient protection.

This she soon discovered when another friend, a soldier, who had long been pursuing her with his attentions, continued to call upon her at the convent, despite her blunt refusals to have anything to do with him. He stubbornly persisted in trying to see her, and, having called at the convent one day about the time of her vision, was greeted with words similar to those with which she had recently dismissed her other visitor.

He made up his mind to get even. Once again, we remind the reader that we are in the thirteenth century – the Middle Ages of fact, not of romance.

Lutgarde had been summoned to the house of her sister. She set out with one or two companions. They had gone some distance into the country when they were met by the soldier and a band of armed men. Lutgarde leapt from her horse. The angry knight tried to seize her, but she broke away and ran into the woods while her companions made off in different directions, crying for help. The men did not go after her. Night fell. She wandered all night through the

---

[3] Discede a me, pabulum mortis, nutrimentum facinoris, quoniam ab alio amatore praeventa sum (*Vita*, 192 b).

woods until finally toward dawn she came upon the house of a friend, her old nurse.

The news had already traveled through the countryside and into the town. Lutgarde spent several days in her refuge: But when the time came for her to return to St. Catherine's, at the edge of the town of St. Trond, there were not only the knight and his henchmen, but a large crowd of curious onlookers, all the idlers and beggars that usually congregated about the gates of a medieval town, together with peddlers, artisans from their shops, and housewives with their busy tongues. Lutgarde's story had been exaggerated by malice and surmise. They were waiting to see her come home.

Seeing the crowd, and knowing what was in their minds, the young girl was filled with embarrassment and fear. But the love of Christ that had begun to burn in her heart was no illusion: and her thoughts turned at once to Him and to the shame He suffered for men, mocked and scourged and stripped and nailed to the cross to die. So Lutgarde, who had been riding veiled, raised her hand and uncovered her face, and showed herself to the world.

Incidents such as these were bound to have a tremendous effect in the soul of a young girl of fifteen. They were to be an important factor in hastening her sanctification.

On her return to the convent, in defiance of the relaxed traditions and customs of the house, she cut herself off entirely from her worldly friends and acquaintances, imposing upon herself a voluntary rule of enclosure and solitude in order to give herself entirely to God.

Immediately the other sisters in the community began to resent her action because of the unfavorable light it cast upon their own lives. They adopted a superior air toward the young oblate, and told her patronizingly that she was just going through a "phase," which would eventually pass off, and she would have the humiliation of returning to the normal way of life led by decent people, whose harmless recreations and friendships she had been so proud as to despise.[4]

Lutgarde entered upon a period of loneliness and difficulties, with frequent temptations to discouragement. Thomas of Cantimpré indicates that, in isolating herself from the ways of her sisters, she had cut off all sources of purely human comfort and sympathy. She wanted to be left alone with God. She was, indeed, left alone. Yet, though she seems to have been fairly constantly aware of God's presence, and to have walked always in His sight, closely united to Him, the union was not close enough to exclude many fears. Hers was a state in which God seemed close — but always just out of reach: a state of peace and yet of anguish, often aggravated by external trials. It is what St. John of the Cross calls the "night of the senses."[5]

This elementary mystical state of purification is common enough: but the extraordinary graces with which it was varied, in Lutgarde's case, are reserved for those for whom God has some special mission among men. Besides a vision of our Lady, we read of St. Catherine, virgin and martyr, appearing to Lutgarde to comfort her in an hour of fear. When Lutgarde's life was nearing its end, and she lay on her deathbed, she related to Thomas of Cantimpré how St. Catherine had prophesied she would never fall into carnal sin. Lutgarde would find a place, in heaven, among the choirs of the virgins.

The scene with the soldier must have been haunting Lutgarde all this time. What might have been a great evil had

---

[4] Cumque nonnullae aemulae arctiorem ejus vitam carperent, quam non poterant imitari; dixerunt: Sinite eam adhuc, dum fervor in cursu est: postea videbitis, cum tepuerit, illam cum rubore repetere, quae nunc stulta contemnit (Vita, 192 e).

[5] Cf. St. John of the Cross, Ascent of Mount Carmel, passim; Dark Night of the Soul, Bk. 1, etc.

turned out to be a great grace. Without it, Lutgarde might have gone on like the other nuns, leading an indifferent life, never falling, perhaps, into any serious sin, but throwing away both time and grace in trivial and purely human pastimes foreign to her vocation. Now, however, she was frightened: and her fear made her pray, and made her unable to refuse Christ any sacrifice. She would do anything to prove that her love for God was sincere.

She undertook many extra penances, fasting beyond the measure of the rest, and spending much of the night in prayer. The jealousy of her sisters was growing. They spied on her, seeking evidence that she was guided not by God but by the devil.

But God multiplied miraculous favors, that the fervor of the young oblate and her zeal for prayer and penance might bear the stamp of His approval. Once, some nuns came upon her alone at prayer in the middle of the night, and found her filled with a vivid radiance that poured out of her body and not only dazzled their eyes but filled their souls with a sweet and sensible grace. Another time, on the Feast of Pentecost, when the *Veni Creator Spiritus* was intoned in choir, at Tierce, Lutgarde was suddenly lifted two cubits from the floor, and left floating in the air on the wings of some unseen spiritual power. Thomas of Cantimpré explains that her body had thus been granted a momentary share in the privileges of her spirit, because of the fact that her soul had already arrived at a high degree of purity and union with God.[6]

Her intimate familiarity with God is illustrated by what might seem to some a rather presumptuous or cavalier attitude in expressing her likes and dislikes to Him, in the matter of

[6] He adds a comment which might serve as an ejaculatory prayer in honor of the saint: *Felix Lutgardis, cujus corpus et anima exultaverunt in Deum vivum!* — "Happy Lutgarde, who exulted, body and soul, in the living God" (*Vita*, 193 a).

His extraordinary favors. Having been granted a "power of healing," in which her very touch had the effect of instantly curing the little sicknesses of those who came to her, she found herself beginning to be very busy with those who appealed to her to cure them of their minor ailments. She complained to God of this, assuring Him that it interfered with her prayer: "Why did You go and give me such a grace, Lord? Now I hardly have any time to be alone with You! Take it away, please," and she added, artlessly, "only give me another grace, give me something better!"[7]

"What grace do you want Me to give you, then, in its place?" Christ asked of her.

Lutgarde, being a choir nun, thought it would be very appropriate if she were to be granted a miraculous understanding of Latin, in order that she might have more devotion in reciting the psalms. As matters stood, she did not understand a word of what she said in choir, although she prayed with great fervor of will.

She discovered, to her surprise that, although this grace was granted, it did not have the result she expected. She began to receive many vivid intellectual lights at the Office, and to be illuminated by numerous penetrating intuitions into the meaning of the psalms. But somehow all this left her heart empty and dry. Thomas of Cantimpré's explanation is not as satisfying as it might be. He tells us that it is "mystery that is the mother of devotion, and a hidden meaning is sought after with greater avidity, for what is concealed is regarded with greater reverence."[8] But after all, there are circumstances where understanding not only helps prayer but is essential to it.

It is good that the life of prayer be built on a solid

[7] *Vita*, 193 b.

[8] Reverentia enim velati mysterii mater est devotionis, et res celata avidius quaeritur, et venerabilius absconsa conspicitur (*Vita*, 193 b).

foundation of clear and thoroughly understood convictions and principles, and it must constantly be fed by spiritual reading. Nevertheless, intellectual activity is sterile in prayer if it does not help the affective movement of the will in its search for God.

However, there is a stage in the spirituality of somewhat advanced souls when clear understanding and definite lights and intuitions about God go far beyond the point of diminishing returns. Such souls seldom need to make a formal discursive meditation and they do not seek brilliant ideas or intuitions in prayer. Attention to these things which are good in themselves would only lead the soul away from a more subtle but more perfect enjoyment of a good that is far higher than anything to which we have access by our own natural powers. Unfortunately, since this higher good is essentially obscure and, so to speak, tasteless to our senses and feelings and intellect, our experience of it is more or less negative: that is to say, we do not realize that we have been tasting this "hidden manna" until it is taken away from us, and we become aware of an undefined emptiness and dissatisfaction. Our peace has given place to restlessness, confusion, and pain.

This was, evidently what happened to St. Lutgarde. Her intellectual lights and intuitions, while being very good in themselves, were not good for her, since they turned her mind and will away from the obscure but immediate enjoyment of God, in the depths of her soul. Paradoxically, these penetrating insights into the meaning of the psalms were, in her case, distractions from the far more important and fruitful and supernatural, though obscure, preoccupation of the mind and will with God.[9]

God had granted her this relatively useless favor together

[9] For a complete exposition of this doctrine on the role of the intellect in contemplative prayer, cf. St. John of the Cross, *Ascent of Mount Carmel,*

with enough light to see that it was not what she needed, and she soon turned to Him once more confessing that all these lofty intuitions only interfered with her devotion instead of nourishing it.[10]

So Jesus asked her: "What, then, do you want?"

This time, Jesus had led her secretly to the discovery of the right answer.

"Lord," she told Him, "I want *Thy Heart*."

"What do you mean: you want My Heart?" said Jesus: "*I* want *your* heart."

Lutgarde replied: "Take it, dear Lord. But take it in such a way that Thy Heart's love may be so mingled and united with my own heart that I may possess my heart in Thee, and may it ever remain there secure in Thy protection."[11]

Here, expressed in simple, imaginative terms, we have a definition of the mystical marriage that sums up St. Bernard's teaching on the subject — and, indeed, the doctrine of all the

---

Bk. II; *Living Flame of Love*, Str. III, verse. 3. No one should ever make the mistake of confusing this teaching on the limitations of the intellect in the higher forms of prayer with quietism, which preached the cessation of every activity of both intellect and will even by beginners in the ways of prayer. Christian mysticism never preaches total inactivity, but the cessation of *natural and human* activity on the part of the faculties in the case of advanced souls, to permit the Holy Ghost to lead them by the path of higher and more obscure and totally supernatural love. See also below, p. 93.

[10] Quid mihi idiotae et rusticae et Laicae Moniali Scripturae secreta cognoscere? (*Vita*, 193 c.) The term *Laica monialis* throws no light on her situation in the convent, except to confirm the word *mancipatur* above. She definitely calls herself *monialis* — nun. The addition of the word *laica* does not mean lay sister, since she was a member of the choir. The Bollandist editor of the *Vita* points out that it simply means "unlettered," "uneducated."

[11] Ita sit, Domine: sed tamen sic ut cordis tui amorem cordi meo contemperes et in te cor meum possideam: omni tempore tuo munimine jam securum (*Vita*, 193 c).

Contempero is a word often used in a technical sense of mixing ingredients in a compound according to their proper proportions: cf. Forcellini, *Lexicon*.

greatest Christian mystical theologians concerning this perfect union of wills.

We observe, first of all, that though the union is so perfect that two wills, two loves have merged into one and the same love, nevertheless the two whose wills are united, the human soul and God, remain ever really and absolutely distinct. Hence, although this is the most perfect union that exists between two separate subsisting beings, it falls infinitely short of the union of Persons in one nature which make the Father, Son, and Holy Ghost One from all eternity. However, the union between the soul and God in love is so close and so complete that the only remaining distinction between them is the fundamental distinction between two separate substances. Otherwise they are identical: that is to say, the soul has "become one with God," and God has "become one with the soul," and the only distinction that remains between them is the fact that what is God's by nature is the soul's by participation and by God's free gift, that is, by love. God *is* love. The soul *has* love. But once the soul reaches transforming union its acts are not only Godlike, but they become *God's own acts*.

Nevertheless, and this is something that is brought out with special clarity in this vision of St. Lutgarde's, these divine acts are not only God's acts, but they belong to the soul as well.

In other words, mystical marriage can never result in the soul's complete absorption in the divine essence to the extent of losing its own essential distinction, its own substantial formality, its subsistence, its personality. On the contrary, it is in this union with God that human personality is finally brought to its highest perfection, its most complete actualization and identity. It is only when we have been transformed "into God" that we become most truly ourselves. Why? Simply because only then are all the deepest potentialities of the soul ultimately and completely fulfilled. This result is the exact opposite of the one arrived at by pantheistic mysticism, which terminates in *nirvana* or total annihilation of personality, individual subsistence, in the one absolute substance.

The closing words of the saint are a plea for the divine protection of the Heart of Christ: a protection that will keep her heart safe in Him and preserve her from all sin. Thomas of Cantimpré gives a charming description of the way in which this prayer was answered. He says that from that time on, Lutgarde rested in the wounded side of Jesus like a baby in her cradle. And Jesus drove away all the temptations that assailed her, just as the nurses in old Brabant used to wave the flies away from the cradles of their infants with fans. From then on Lutgarde was not even assailed by carnal thoughts or images. Her soul was untroubled by the flesh, and remained serene, in union with the Heart of Christ.[12]

St. Lutgarde is perhaps the first saint in whom this mystical "exchange of hearts" was effected. Since her time, the exchange has become rather common in the lives of mystics devoted to the Sacred Heart of Jesus. We read of it in the lives of St. Gertrude, St. Mechtilde (both Cistercians), and St. Margaret Mary. The term is, of course, purely symbolic. There is no question of a physical exchange, but only of a mystical union of wills. Nor does it imply the perfect union of wills in mystical marriage. The exchange of hearts can take place in the degree of union known as spiritual betrothal. The gift then becomes not a sign of perfect transforming union but rather a pledge of that union, which still remains to be desired and which God withholds until His own good time.

[12] In our own time, Sister Josefa Menendez, a lay sister of the Society of the Sacred Heart, received similar grace as a protection against temptations to leave the convent.

CHAPTER TWO

PRIORESS AT ST. CATHERINE'S

THE mystical life of St. Lutgarde had begun with two
striking visions, both of which established her as one
of the first great votaries of the Sacred Heart of Jesus.
To be devoted to the Sacred Heart means to penetrate deeply,
by contemplation and love, into the mystery of the love of
Jesus for men. The perfection of the devotion is reached in a
perfect union with that love — an identification with Christ
which conforms the heart of the saint entirely to His burning
Heart, pierced on Calvary by the lance of Longinus. The way
to this identification is not to be sought anywhere else but in
the Sacred Heart itself. It is from the pierced side of our dying
Saviour that we must seek all the graces that will enable us to
grow in charity until we are consumed with the same humility
and abnegation and love that brought Him to the death of the
Cross. In the end, we must die of love as He died of love for
us. In this death of love is found the perfect fulfillment of life,
for by it we die and "pass over" in the ecstasy of pure love
which transforms us into our God.

Jesus had awakened the heart of Lutgarde to a new life by
showing her His own pierced Heart, which is the fountain
of all grace and all love and all delight. He had even
betrothed her to Himself by an espousal in which she received
His Sacred Heart in exchange for her own heart; that is to
say in which she was raised to a mystical union of love with
Him. This union was still something short of the perfection

16

of mystical marriage. She was not yet transformed into her Beloved so as to become completely one with Him. She still had to be raised out of herself, and lifted up to Him in order to receive from Him the life of her life and the love which was the source of all her love.

While she was still a young girl, before she had made profession with the Benedictine nuns of St. Catherine's, she received another remarkable grace.

Thomas of Cantimpré places this vision in the same period when she experienced the "exchange of hearts." Lutgarde had fallen sick with "a fever." She was in bed, and heard the bell ring for Matins, about two o'clock in the morning. Her head was burning, her flesh shook with chills, and her clothing was wet with perspiration. She thought it would be wise to stay in bed and sleep off her sickness, because it might be dangerous for her to get up and go to choir with the nuns, and stand in the cold church when she was shivering and wet with fever.

Considering her youth and her more or less equivocal position in the religious life, and in a mitigated Order, she was quite entitled to stay in bed. However, she heard the voice of Christ, urging her to rise and go to choir with the others. "Get up, quickly, Lutgarde! Why are you lying there? For at this very hour, sinners are wallowing in the mire of their vices, and you ought to be doing penance for them, instead of lying there and letting your body perspire!"[1] Filled with fear, Lutgarde leapt from her bed and hastened to choir where the Office had already begun. At the door of the Church she saw Christ.

She beheld His living body, nailed to the cross: but the lance wound was open in His side. As she approached Him, Christ let down one of His arms from the Cross to embrace

[1] Surge cito: quid jaces? Oportet te modo pro peccatoribus, qui in suis jacent sudoribus, poenitentiam agere, non indulgere sudori . . . (*Vita*, 193 d).

her and draw her to Himself. As He did so, He pressed her lips to the bleeding wound in His side, and from His Sacred Heart the young nun drew forth a mighty current of spiritual power which filled her with fortitude and joy. And from then on, says Thomas, her lips distilled, as it were, milk and honey: that is to say, she constantly meditated upon the honey of Christ's divinity and the milk of His humanity, which she ever tasted in the depths of her soul.

Is it necessary to repeat that, although this was an imaginary vision, or one which she beheld through the medium of a phantasm, nevertheless the embrace, and kiss, all belong to the spiritual and mystical, not to the material order? To say that she "drank from the pierced side of Christ" is simply to indicate that she received a strong infusion of the grace merited for men by His Passion and death.

On the other hand, so far as she herself was concerned, this was a tremendously real, emotional experience, striking deep into the very substance of her soul, it is true, but at the same time working strongly upon the interior senses. So, while the word *mystical*, applied to such an experience, by no means signifies "unreal" or "merely symbolic," we must not go to the other extreme and reduce it to a miraculous interference in the purely material order, as though she were literally "drinking" from the spear-wound in the side of Christ.

In her first vision, Lutgarde had been promised the knowledge of all that was worthy of love, if she would turn aside from creatures and concern herself with the Heart of Jesus alone. She had been granted, if not the perfection of mystical marriage, at least what practically amounted to impeccability with regard to the sixth and ninth commandments. Now she had been privileged to draw, from that same Heart, the fortitude of the martyrs. It was not surprising that, with all these graces, she came close to the "Apostle whom Jesus loved" and who had rested his head upon our Lord's breast at the Last Supper. St. John the Evangelist has always, for obvious reasons, been closely associated with devotion to the Sacred Heart: in some ways, he has rather suffered by this association at the hands of third-rate pious artists who have done a great disservice to Christianity by their mawkish caricatures of the tender but virile love of the saints for their God.

St. Lutgarde, like all true mystics, had enough purity of soul to be lifted above the plane of sentimentality to that of genuine charity. No doubt the great Apostle took part in this, by his powerful intercession. In any case his interest in her spiritual progress was manifested to her by a vision of him in the form of an eagle. This vision was intellectual in its character, the substance of its meaning being translated into imaginative and human terms after it had already been impressed, supernaturally, upon her intellect.

The eagle, according to the usual tradition of medieval bestiaries, had the most piercing vision of all creatures, and was supposed to be able to stare straight into the sun without blinking. Also, its powerful wings were able to carry it higher into the heavens than any other bird. It was an obvious symbol of mystical contemplation.

In this particular vision, St. Lutgarde saw the "Eagle of Patmos" flying with plumage that so blazed with light that the whole world could have been illuminated by the glory of his wings. Touching her lips with his beak, the "Eagle" instantly filled her with a flood of such intense intellectual light that it seemed there could be no secret of the divine essence that still lay hid to her.

Thomas of Cantimpré testifies that although her speech was plain, and her explanations colloquial and totally unscientific, St. Lutgarde was able to set forth the highest truths of theology with a wisdom, and subtlety, and accuracy that simply took his breath away — indeed, he declares her burning, lucid words were able to kindle the fires of an almost ecstatic intuition in his own soul.[2]

We also read of her, at this time, visiting a recluse at Loos — a fact that has nothing very extraordinary about it. The Low-countries and Germany were swarming with pious women who had consecrated themselves to God in this solitary state, and they were frequently visited and consulted by religious, clergy, and laity. Religious women would sometimes spend a week or two in the cell of a recluse, praying and conversing about spiritual things. We read of such a visit in the life of Bl. Ida of Louvain, before she became a Cistercian nun.[3]

However, this recluse was later to bear witness to the fact that St. Lutgarde, when in ecstasy, was so overpowered by divine joy that she seemed like one intoxicated with bliss, and could not contain her exclamations and cries and movements that betrayed the might of the rapture that possessed her. This mystical jubilation is something that has been discussed by many writers, not the least authoritative being Cassian, who had observed it among the anchorites of Egypt.[4] It seems

[2] Licet ipsa in communibus verbis, rudis quodammodo et simplicissima videretur et esset; tamen numquam ab ore alicujus ita sincera, ita ardentissima, ita secundum veritatis spiritum decisa verba, in spiritualis collationis secretis inveni; in tantum ut rudem me prorsus et hebetem ad intellectum verborum ejus saepissime reputarem. Loci adhuc et temporis memor, tantum me aliquando in verborum ejus subtilitate stupuisse profiteor; ut si diu me illa dulcis et ineffabilis admiratio tenuisset aut amentem me utique, aut extinctum penitus reddidisset (*Vita*, 194 b).

"Although she spoke in the language of the common people, and seemed, as indeed she was, uneducated and simple, yet never have I heard from the lips of anyone words so sincere, so full of fire, so vivid in their expression of the spirit of truth as she often told me in confidence, in spiritual direction. Indeed it often happened that I was amazed at my own ignorance and incapacity to plumb the depths of her full meaning. I remember one occasion when the subtlety of her words so completely stunned me that I am certain that if that sweet and inexpressible ecstasy of wonder had held sway over me for long, I would have gone out of my mind, or indeed been killed by it on the very spot."

[3] Cf. *Acta Sanctorum*, April, ii, 176.
[4] *Conferences* IX, 27. Migne, P. L., 49:803.

to have been common among Flemish mystics. Bl. Arnulph, the amazing Cistercian lay brother of Villers, had also been granted this blessing — or, perhaps in his case, it was more of an affliction than a blessing.[5]

No less a grace than all of these, but one which is accessible to all souls with the ordinary assistance of God, was that of religious profession. Lutgarde made her vows, some time about 1200, in the presence of the Bishop of Liége, who placed upon her head and those of the other nuns who were professed together with her, small crowns or circlets of linen. One of the bystanders was convinced that he saw Lutgarde receiving a crown of gold, and one of the nuns had the same impression. Later events proved that they were not wrong in their interpretation of the experience, whether vision or pious fancy, as presage of her sanctity.

If St. Lutgarde had made her profession as a Trappistine in our own day, she would have been crowned with flowers.

From then on, she continued with even greater fervor in her life of prayer and austerity and charity. This included a strong insistence on neglected points of the Rule, like manual labor, as well as many penances and fasts that were not only far beyond the Rule, but struck Thomas of Cantimpré as being beyond the strength of the men of his time.[6] This is particularly interesting in view of the fact that most Benedictine monasteries of the time, although observing great latitude in the quantity and quality of food served in their refectories, did nevertheless more or less observe the times prescribed by St. Benedict for meals — which meant waiting until Vespers before the only meal of the day in Lent. This alone would be considered, by many, beyond the strength of the men of our own time, but it was common among the faithful of the Middle Ages.

[5] Cf. *Acta Sanctorum*, June, vii 1, 570.

[6] *Vita*, 194 d. She spent her "whole life," he says, in these superhuman fasts.

Although, as we have seen, a certain amount of envy and comment had been excited by Lutgarde's intense fervor, it seems that in the course of her nine years in the convent, everyone had been forced to acknowledge not only her sanctity of life, but her eminent fitness to be Superioress of the house.

In any case, Lutgarde was elected prioress. In fact, she was elected unanimously[7] — a thing which is rather surprising, in view of the envy of which she had once been the object. The Bollandists place this event about the year 1205, when the saint was twenty-three years old.

Far from being flattered or pleased by her elevation to this dignity, Lutgarde regarded it as a disaster.[8] Indeed, it seems to have moved her to look elsewhere, and to seek some other Order, as if she thought St. Catherine's could provide her with sufficient opportunities for living as a contemplative as long as she was an obscure member of the community but not when she took her place at its head.

It was natural that her thoughts should turn to the austere Cistercian nuns, who had, by this time, many flourishing convents in the Low Countries. It was over a century since St. Robert had left the monastery of Molesme with St. Alberic and St. Stephen Harding to found the abbey of Citeaux, the cradle of the greatest Benedictine reform of the Middle Ages. The first half of the twelfth century had seen the almost miraculous diffusion of the Cistercian monks over every part of the Christian world. Although the fathers of the Order had at first resolved to have nothing to do with the direction of religious women, a convent founded at Tart, near Dijon, and therefore in the vicinity of Citeaux, adopted the Cistercian Rule, and eventually the Order took

---

[7] Uno omnium consensu (*Vita*, 195 e).

[8] Quia gravissimam sibi in hoc factam injuriam aestimabat, mutare ex tunc locum et propositum disponebat (*Vita*, 195 e).

these nuns under its jurisdiction. Although the growth of this branch of the Cistercian family was not quite so rapid, the Cistercian nuns attracted many vocations in the Low Countries, northern France, and western Germany, regions which were then at the very peak of a strong religious movement which owed its origin, in part, to the basic upheaval of society resulting from the emergence of the new, powerful bourgeois class of artisans and merchants in the great free cities and communes.

This social ferment had brought about certain radical modifications in the position of women in society, liberating them, in large numbers, from their condition of almost total dependence and quasi-servitude, and enabling them to give expression to the deep religious needs of their souls by consecrating themselves to God as Beguines, recluses, or nuns — a privilege which had been, hitherto, far more limited. The Beguines were especially numerous, since their condition required no dowry. We read that there were some two hundred thousand Beguines in Germany. The city of Cambrai had thirteen hundred of them in the year 1240, and Nivelles sheltered two thousand.[9]

So great was to be the affluence of women to the Cistercian Order that the General Chapter of 1228[10] finally forbade the foundation of any more convents, or the admission of any already founded, into the Order.

Had the mendicant orders come into existence, St. Lutgarde might have had some hesitation in making a choice — although the Poor Clares and the Dominican nuns never held the dominant position that was exercised by the Cistercians in the Low Countries. As matters stood, there was little likelihood of her becoming a recluse, and there was no

[9] Figures taken from Th. Plogaerts, *Histoire de l'abbaye d'Aywières*, p. vii.
[10] Canivez, *Statuta Capituli Generalis Ordinis Cisterciensis*, 1228, No. 16, Vol. ii, p. 68.

incentive for one under religious vows to adopt the quasi-religious life of a Beguine, which would have been equivalent to a return to the world.

The Cistercian nuns, on the other hand (like the White Monks), had astounded their age by the austerity of their life, by the rigor of their poverty, penance, and fasting, by their isolation and their lives of prayer — and to all this the reputation and mystical writings of St. Bernard and other great speculative mystics of the twelfth century had imparted an aureola of glory. To the men and women of the twelfth century, the bare Cistercian monasteries and convents, isolated in their remote valleys and silent forests, spoke not only of stern mortification and rigorous penances, but, above all, of opportunities to ascend the heights of mystical contemplation and arrive at perfect union with God. When Dante sought a guide to introduce him, in the final circles of paradise, into the full glory of the vision of the divine essence, he found no one more worthy than St. Bernard of Clairvaux, and this is enough to show what the Cistercian Order meant in Europe down to the end of the thirteenth century.

Another reason for the veneration in which the Order was held was the debt which Christian Europe realized it owed to the White Monks who had brought them under the sovereignty of the glorious Virgin Mother of God, the Queen of heaven and earth. Mary had been loved and venerated, indeed, in the earlier centuries of the Church, but never until the twelfth century had she been brought so close to men. Never before had men realized the splendor of her glory as the Virgin Mother of God: never before had they realized the might of her universal intercession, the power of her loving prayers over the Heart of the divine Child who now appeared everywhere in her arms. Never before had they realized how much she loved them, and wanted to help them, for her delights were to be with the sons of men.[11] It was the White Monks, especially St. Bernard, who presented the Queen of Heaven to the world not as a remote and cloudy figure beyond the stars, but as our liege Lady, than whose service there is no greater glory because she is Mother of God and because to serve her is to serve Christ, who willed that all should come to Him through Mary, inasmuch as He willed all graces to come to us through her.[12] It is not surprising that St. Lutgarde should be attracted by the Cistercian life. Her only problem lay in the choice of a convent.

She asked the advice of a learned preacher of Liége, Jean de Lierre, who urged her to give up her post as prioress and leave the Benedictine Order for the Cistercian convent of Aywières, which had recently been founded near Liége, but had been transferred to a site in Brabant, near the village of Lillois, where it was now under the jurisdiction of the White Monks of Villers.

She was very reluctant to accept this particular choice, because French was spoken in Brabant, and she felt it would be unwise to enter a convent where she would not understand the language of her superiors or spiritual directors. For her own part, Lutgarde preferred the Cistercian convent of Herkenrode, in her own country, where Flemish was spoken. Herkenrode, as a matter of fact, had been the first foundation of Cistercian nuns in Belgium, and it was situated only a few miles from St. Trond. In its twenty years of existence it had become more firmly established than the unsettled community of Aywières. Later on, it was to become one of the most famous places of Pilgrimage in Belgium, and one of its most splendid and important abbeys. The center

[11] Deliciae meae esse cum filiis hominum (Prov. 8:31), Epistle for the Feast of the Immaculate Conception.

[12] Cf. St. Bernard's famous sermon "De Aquaeductu" — *in Nativitate B. V. Mariae.*

of attraction there was to be the Miraculous Host, which is still venerated in our own time, in the church of St. Quentin at Hasselt.

This Host was one which, having been taken by a priest to a sick person, had been touched by profane hands while his back was turned, and had immediately shown miraculous drops of blood. Conveyed secretly to the church of the Cistercian nuns at Herkenrode, its passage was marked by more miracles, and when, upon arriving, the Host was deposited upon the altar, all who were present visibly beheld Christ before them crowned with thorns. For centuries the faithful received great graces in answer to their prayers at this shrine, and when the nuns were expelled during the French revolution the Host, still marvelously preserved, was hidden in a tin box walled into the kitchen of a private house. Afterward it was withdrawn and placed in its present abode.

None of this, however, was to happen until more than a hundred years after the time St. Lutgarde was debating about her vocation.[13]

Meanwhile, Christ Himself intervened, and spoke the following words to her: "It is My will that you go to Aywières, and if you do not go, I will have nothing more to do with you."[14]

As if this were not enough, Lutgarde was also admonished by a saintly friend, since venerated as St. Christine "the

[13] The miraculous Host was enshrined at Herkenrode in 1317. The abbey was founded in 1182. In the period of the decline of the Cistercian Order it grew in size and wealth until it attained the proportions of a small town. Its church was decorated with splendid works of art and possessed (contrary to the ancient rules of the Order) some fine stained-glass windows which, after the French revolution, were bought and set up in the Anglican cathedral of Lichfield, Staffordshire. Cf. Canivez, *Ordre de Citeaux en Belgique*, p. 124 ff.

[14] Volo ut ad locum Aquiriae finaliter pergas, et nisi facias, ego te deseram (*Vita*, 195 c).

Admirable,"[15] to go to Aywières and so with no further possibility of doubt as to the convent of the Cistercian Order to which she was called, Lutgarde left St. Catherine's without consulting her community and went to Aywières.

When the nuns of St. Catherine's discovered their loss, they were inconsolable, but it was too late to do anything about it. Lutgarde, in her turn, prayed earnestly for the peace of the community she had left and was assured by the Blessed Virgin that her prayers would be answered. Indeed, Thomas of Cantimpré ends the first book of his life of St. Lutgarde with the comment: "The indubitable effect of these prayers is to be seen even today [some fifty years later] in the community of St. Catherine's. For this particular convent continues to grow in fervor more than ever, and to increase, at the same time, in temporal prosperity."[16]

[15] The life of St. Christine was also written by Thomas of Cantimpré, and *mirabilis* — amazing, or astounding — is a weak word for it. Her fantastic career really began when she "died." At the funeral service, her body not only came to life, but took flight, soared out of the coffin and alighted on one of the beams, high in the roof of the church. The building was almost instantly emptied of all its occupants except Christine, her sister, and the priest saying Mass, who, when he had finished, ordered her to come down, and was obeyed. Later on, these flights were so frequently repeated that her family, believing her to be in the power of evil spirits, hired a strong man to seize her and hold her down when she started to rise off the ground. Finding that this guardian was usually unable to catch her in time, they chained her to the wall, then chained her in a sealed room, from which she escaped. Her favorite place of prayer was in the tops of tall trees, and she was called the "flying saint." Cf. Nimal, *Grandes Saintes du Pays de Liége*, p. 102 ff., and *Acta Sanctorum*, July 24. Unbelievable as these stories seem, they are supposed to have been corroborated by many witnesses and vouched for by sober and learned men of the time. She was a precursor of St. Joseph of Cupertino!

[16] *Vita*, 195 e.

CHAPTER THREE

AYWIÈRES. THE ALBIGENSIANS. HER FIRST SEVEN YEAR FAST.

WE DO not know whether St. Lutgarde entered Aywières before or after its second change of site. But in any case, the convent finally settled upon its permanent location at Couture Saint-Germain, and it was there that Lutgarde spent the rest of the years of her life in relative seclusion. We say relative because, as will be seen, the fame of her mystical gifts and of her great sanctity brought many visitors to the convent, men and women of all levels of society, seeking her prayers and her inspired advice. Nevertheless, it was a great improvement over St. Catherine's, for here she was protected by the strictest enclosure, spent most of her time in complete silence, and was relieved of all the responsibilities of office in the community. At last she could give herself, as she desired, to prayer and penance.

The valley of Aywières is, even today, a beautiful, secluded site in the open country southwest of Brussels. Indeed, it is on the confines of the great battlefield of Waterloo — pleasant, rolling country, full of meadows and fertile fields, interspersed with woods and farms, watered by streams lined with tall, graceful popular trees. In this quiet place some buildings of the convent and the old enclosure wall still stand despite the ravages of centuries of war that have occasionally submerged the valley in dark waves of terror and destruction.

Behind the white walls of this Cistercian convent, dedicated to the Mother of God, Lutgarde had at last found the life she was seeking. Here a community of women did not fear to give themselves to God in the full rigor of the Cistercian Usages as they were lived by the monks of Citeaux and Clairvaux and Villers and several hundred other monasteries in every part of Europe. Every night, between one and two o'clock, they rose to chant the canonical office, and then, on most days of the year, to chant the office of the dead. After that, in the cold hour before dawn, they sat in the cloister or Chapter Room reading, by the light of candles. Then came Lauds, in winter, Prime in summer, followed by chapter — and severe penances were often imposed at the chapter of faults. It was not uncommon for one to receive the discipline on her bare shoulders from another member of the community. In the wintertime the nuns went to work after Tierce and High Mass, and the work continued until the first bell for None, with a break for the office of Sext, recited in the fields if they were outside the monastery. After None, about two in the afternoon, the only meal of the day was taken, in the winter season. In summer the work was divided, ending at Sext, when dinner was taken, and was followed by a short rest in the dormitory, and work continued in the afternoon. In winter, however, after dinner the nuns devoted themselves to reading or prayer until Vespers. After Vespers, supper was taken in the summer, and in winter, instead of the light collation at present given in the Order, there were simply "*biberes*" — a drink of wine or small beer. In the late afternoon the *collatio* or public reading in the cloister was held, while the daylight still lingered on. Then Compline was sung and the nuns retired to their hard couch of boards and straw, in a common dormitory where they did not enjoy the privacy of partitioned cells as they do today.

The life was much the same, in its broad outlines, as life in a Trappist monastery or convent of Trappistines in our day, except that while the fasts were stricter and longer, eggs and fish were occasionally served in the refectory. The Little Office of the Blessed Virgin was not, at this time, recited in choir, but in the infirmary chapel. Communion was less frequent throughout the Church in the Middle Ages, and it is almost impossible to find out how often the nuns received the Holy Eucharist. They generally did not enjoy the privilege of daily Communion. The *Consuetudines* or Usages of the first Cistercians encouraged weekly Communion, and prescribed it on certain great feasts. We may say that the maximum frequency in receiving the Blessed Sacrament known in the Church in the Middle Ages was encouraged in the Cistercian Order.

The liturgy was far simpler than today, and the entire office was sung every day. Our first Fathers were extremely strict in their insistence that no decorations that savored of display or excited mere natural curiosity should find a place in Cistercian churches. Accordingly the choirs and sanctuaries of our ancient monasteries, in the golden age of the Order, were extremely simple and austere. We need only remark that nowhere in our Order, since the time when the Rules laid down for us by our Fathers in the matter of liturgical simplicity were put aside, have we ever had a mystic of the caliber of St. Lutgarde, Bl. Ida of Nivelles, St. Gertrude, St. Mechtilde, still less of St. Aelred or St. Bernard.

What was the reason for this great austerity of life?

The first Cistercians had been very simple and matter of fact in their statement of their aims: they said they wanted to keep the Rule of St. Benedict to the letter, but they did not theorize very much about their ultimate reasons for doing so. Rather, they concentrated upon expressing, in the clearest possible terms, just what they understood by keeping the Rule to the letter, and what this might involve.

From the legislation sketched out in the *Exordium Parvum*

we gather that the aim of the first Cistercians was to strip
the Benedictine life of all the useless accretions and mitigations
it had picked up in the course of centuries, and return to the
pure ideal of the great Patriarch of the West. This may be
summed up as: a life devoted entirely to the service of Christ,
by complete self-renunciation, through the means of total
obedience in the spirit of faith, to a superior, and by the public
work of adoration, the Divine Office or *Opus Dei*. St.
Bernard seems to have found the ultimate expression of
Benedictinism in the last lines of the Chapter on Humility in
the Holy Rule.

Here, Benedict tells us that the monk, "having ascended
all these degrees of humility, arrives at that love of God
which perfectly casts out all fear. And through this love he
shall then begin to follow all the observances, which before
he kept not without fear [that is, which he had to *force
himself to keep* for fear of the loss of his soul, or of falling
into his old, sinful habits], he shall begin to follow all these
observances without any difficulty or repugnance, and as it
were naturally, and with the ease of an acquired habit, *no
longer impelled by the fear of hell, but by the love of Christ*
and the good habit he has developed, and by the delight he
now takes in virtue as such."[1]

In other words, St. Bernard viewed the Benedictine life
as a life of pure love for God: a life in which penance and
mortification are essential because of our need to strip our-

---

[1] Ergo his omnibus humilitatis gradibus ascensis, monachus mox ad
charitatem Dei perveniet illam, quae perfecta foris mittit timorem; per
quam universa quae prius non sine formidine observabat, absque ullo
labore, velut naturaliter ex consuetudine incipiet custodire, non jam
timore gehennae, sed amore Christi et consuetudine ipsa bona, et delecta-
tione virtutum (*Regula*, cap. vii, circ. fin). Etienne Gilson (*The Mystical
Theology of St. Bernard*, p. 28) points out how the mysticism of the saint
of Clairvaux is built on the foundation of St. Benedict's Rule, especially in
its teachings on obedience and humility, and that the passage just quoted
was of cardinal importance in this matter.

selves of all that self-will and self-love which are irrevocably opposed to the love of God, and which are the source of all fear, all ignorance, all sin, all misery in our lives, because they separate us from Him who alone is our happiness. The best means of accomplishing this work of purification is always obedience, the community life, manual labor and the regular observance of the Rule. The fundamental positive expression of our love for God is the adoration of Him, in union with Christ and the saints and angels and the whole Church, in the Divine Office and Holy Mass: but this must necessarily be completed by the monks' private prayer, his constant affective union with God in all that he does, his intervals of meditative reading (*Lectio Divina*) and contemplation.

If it was not altogether clear in the Rule that the monk was destined to lead a life of contemplative and even mystical union with God, by love, St. Bernard and the Cistercian theologians of his school made it very evident that this was the perfection of the monastic life as they conceived it.[2]

It was this ideal of a life of love for God "without measure" that attracted St. Lutgarde to the Cistercian cloister. And she, as a matter of fact, was to add something of her own to the mysticism of St. Bernard.

The ideal of vicarious suffering, as a most excellent and perfect expression of our love for God, had not been developed in St. Bernard — or indeed in any of the Fathers before him — to the refined pitch which it was to acquire in mystics of more modern times, beginning especially in the age of St. Lutgarde, with her and other Cistercians, with St. Francis of Assisi and his followers, later with the great Carmelite St. Teresa, but most explicitly with St. Margaret Mary and,

---

[2] Cf. William of St. Thierry's opening chapter, bk. I, c. i, of the Epistle to the Brethren of Mont Dieu (Migne, *P. L.*, 184); St. Bernard, *In Cantica, passim*, but especially Sermons 31–34; the final sermons of the same series, etc., cf. Gilson, *op. cit.*, Chaps. i and iv, especially p. 91.

in our own times, in St. Gemma Galgani, St. Thérèse of Lisieux, and Theresa Neumann.

There are few saints in the history of the Church in whom the ideal of vicarious suffering in reparation for sin was better developed than in St. Lutgarde: and this development really began to reach its full scope when she entered Aywières and became a Cistercian nun.

But before we go on to consider the form this life of suffering and reparation was to take, we must pause to consider the social conditions which were its occasion.

There were many reasons why scholastic philosophy and Catholic theology reached so high a peak of perfection in the thirteenth century. One of the most important factors in this development was the presence of several widespread and tenacious heresies which called for the formation of such an Order as that which was soon to be founded by St. Dominic: an Order devoted to preaching and to the teaching of the sacred sciences.

This will surprise no one: but what may seem more astonishing to many is the fact that an obscure contemplative nun, in a newly founded Cistercian convent in Brabant, was destined by God to play an important part in the struggle against heresy without ever leaving the enclosure of her convent. St. Lutgarde's life of penance and reparation was explicitly aimed at the Albigensian heresy.

The term *Albigensian* is sometimes taken as a generic designation for all the heresies derived from manichaeism, that flourished in France and Italy and Germany in the twelfth and thirteenth centuries. Perhaps the word *Catharist* is more accurate, since it suggests the principles common to all these groups, while the Albigensians, properly speaking, were only the Cathari who flourished in Languedoc. Albi was not the cradle of the heresy by any means. It would be hard to say just where it did come from. The embers of manichaeism

and gnosticism and of many other heresies had been smolder-
ing for several centuries, and no doubt contact with the East
in the crusades had done much to revive their flame.

Then, too, society was ready for these movements. The
breakdown of the feudal system and the growth of the communes had created a large, vigorous, and independent class
of artisans and merchants, who looked out upon the world
about them with an avid curiosity and interest that did not
aspire to the learning of the schools, but did, definitely, demand some kind of popular philosophy and theology — some
answer to ultimate questions about life. This hunger could
no longer be satisfied merely by the liturgy of the Church. The
fault was not with the liturgy: it lay in the fact that society
had developed in such a way that the men of the towns, torn
away from the harmonious and integrated round of life in
which the liturgy and seasons moved together, had lost the
deep liturgical sense possessed by an earlier generation and
had acquired, in its stead, a vaguely speculative curiosity
which was shallow, no doubt, but nonetheless real.

This curiosity was inevitable, and it was a good thing. But
it needed to be satisfied by good preaching in the churches,
by solid religious instruction. Another thing that was needed
was a strong sacramental life among Christians: but that
life was weak in the medieval Church. Frequent Communion was almost unknown, and there were very few
priests who said Mass daily. Many did not offer the Holy
Sacrifice more than once a week, and some did so even less
frequently. Thousands of the faithful had never been confirmed, never received their First Communion.

We think of the Middle Ages as a time when the minds
of all men were very much alive to the truths of faith. That
is not quite accurate. Men lived in the atmosphere of a
strongly Christian culture, and their minds and hearts were
deeply imbued with Christian traditions, and their souls were

wonderfully well disposed to believe in God and to love Him. Nevertheless belief all too often degenerated into credulity, while sometimes the fundamental dogmas of the faith were not known. St. Peter of Tarentaise found many in his mountain diocese in twelfth-century France who had not only not been confirmed but had never heard of the Holy Ghost.[3]

It was an age of extremes, and we must not let the large number of great saints blind us to the large number of heretics and simoniacs and schismatics and apostates.

The newly formed populations that fermented in the rising communes received little or no solid Christian teaching. Preaching was reserved to bishops, as a rule. There was certainly no such thing as a regular Sunday sermon by the parish priest.[4]

As they lost contact with the Church and its liturgical life, men met with little to satisfy their craving for knowledge of ultimate truths, unless they happened to belong to the minority that could intelligently follow the discussions of the schools, in cities like Paris, Bologna, or Oxford.

There was left a large undefined group of half-educated men gathering in the communes, men with active and curious minds, and souls avid for religious experience, who were ready to fall a prey to anyone who appealed to them with new and convincing arguments. In this intellectual half-world were many charlatans, and many sincere but misguided men as well: and the combination of ignorance, desire of truth, intellectual dishonesty, and erroneous consciences bred several great heresies, the worst of which was that of the Cathari.

If Catharism spread rapidly because of the opening of many new minds to curiosity and speculation, at least on an elementary level, that does not mean that its appeal was primarily intellectual. On the contrary, perhaps the two

---

[3] *Acta Sanctorum*, May, ii, p. 323.
[4] Cf. Mandonnet, St. *Dominic and His Work*.

greatest reasons for its success were its pseudo-mystical character and its fierce, unbalanced asceticism. Again, it was ad-
mirably fitted to spread rapidly and efficiently because it was
controlled by a minority, an elite of supremely energetic,
sincere, and uncompromising zealots, who influenced others
as much by example as by word.

This minority was the sect of the Cathari properly so
called. They were the initiates, the elect, the real devotees
of the heretical religion. They alone had undergone the ritual
pseudo-baptism, which was never administered without a
long and strict period of training. They alone had access to
all the doctrines of the sect, most of which were kept secret
from outsiders. The Cathari were not primarily preachers or
propagandists. They depended more on example than on
sermons. If they did preach by word, their preaching was
largely destructive. It was directed against the Church and
her sacramental system.

Perhaps they would never have got men to listen to them,
in their attacks upon the dogmas of the Incarnation, the
Eucharist, the Church, and so on, had they not been able to
level such telling blows against the moral life of the clergy,
and particularly against the avarice and worldly power of
abbots and prelates.

The wealth and pomp and luxury, often the cruelty and
sensuality, of worldly clerics, were a striking contrast to the
tremendously austere life of the Cathari. They practiced
absolute poverty, detested meat, and had a pathological horror
of the flesh and its desires — a horror which was, however,
too unbalanced to save them from falling secretly into the
most hellish corruptions of natural passion.

The doctrines of Catharism are a good illustration of the
extremes to which a misguided and unbalanced religious zeal
can go, when left to its own devices. Eccentricity and sin-
gularity in the religious life can often be traced to clumsily

repressed passion, which breaks out again in some crude disguise which the warped conscience of the victim is too ill-instructed to detect. Anyone with a smattering of modern psychiatry can see what underlay the curiously twisted ascetic and moral doctrines of the Cathari.

The very core of the Catharist's spiritual life was a morbid horror of sex and of the flesh — a horror so extreme as to be scarcely distinguishable from fascination. The whole crazy framework of Catharistic doctrine is built on this horror. They believed that the flesh, man's body, and all material creation were absolutely evil and filthy. All this had been created by the devil, whom they had elevated to the rank of first principle in his own right, in the order of evil, as God is the first principle in the order of good. Thus evil became something positive, a real entity. Between this entity and the good entity was waged an eternal conflict. Men had been caught in the middle of this cosmic upheaval by the fall. The souls of men were really fallen angels, imprisoned, as a punishment, in impure human bodies and immersed in the filth of material creation.

Rescue from this state had been effected for them by the Son of God, the Christ of the New Testament: but Christ had never really taken flesh, since the flesh was filthy. Therefore He had not died or risen from the dead: these doctrines were only illusions. In fact, most of the New Testament was an illusion, and that left them with very little of revelation, since they had previously rejected the Old Testament on the grounds that it was written by the devil. The Cathari were particularly bitter in their attacks on the priesthood and the Sacrifice of the Mass.

Since the flesh was evil, and bodily life was an almost irreparable disaster, the Cathari naturally concluded that marriage was a device of the devil to tighten his grip on that part of the spiritual world which came under his influence, by encouraging the procreation of children and the imprisonment of more souls in flesh. Therefore they taught that no man who persisted in matrimony until death could be saved.

The effects produced by this teaching upon the non-initiated, who were not devoted to the life of uncompromising asceticism of the "elect," may well be imagined! It resulted in an almost total disregard of sexual morality and in the complete disruption of family life. What made it worse was the fact that these misguided men believed that there was no such thing as responsibility for the sins of the flesh: such "sins" were simply the work of the devil. The flesh was entirely under his power, and the soul could not be taxed with them. Man was not free to resist.

Finally, as a culmination to this lunatic outlook on life, came the asceticism of the so-called "perfect." They would not eat meat or eggs or drink milk on the grounds that these things were defiled by animal generation. We do not know the details of their ascetic practices as a means to contemplation, but one may surmise that they were largely a matter of self-hypnotism. Finally, if one of the elect did not manage to get himself into ecstasy by any other means, he was free to liberate his soul from the flesh by committing suicide.

The greatest danger of Catharism lay precisely in its claim to a higher and purer spirituality than that of the Church. All these errors were put forward in the name of an exalted mysticism which alone was capable of bringing man to union with the great spiritual principle of all goodness and truth and light.

Since the devil and our own natural powers are able, by dint of labor and ascetic practices, to produce certain conditions that vaguely resemble mystical states, and which, with the help of our imagination can conjure up sensations of intense interior pleasure, there is no doubt that those who learned the "technique" were intoxicated by the sense of a new and exalted experience, and were convinced that they had at last found the way to sanctity and high contemplation.

The Church had not stood idly by and let the Cathari have everything their own way. But until the time of Innocent III, efforts had been sporadic and poorly co-ordinated. Even that great pontiff had failed at first. He hath summoned contemplative monks from the cloisters of the strongest and most fervent Order then in the Church to fight the heresy. But the mission of Cistercian abbots and monks which went to preach in Languedoc at the Pope's command had no success. It was not the vocation of White Monks to preach in the world. Rather it was the blood of the Cistercian martyr, Bl. Peter of Castelnau, that helped prepare the way for those whom God Himself was raising up to overcome the heresy: St. Dominic and his austere Order of Preachers, vowed to lives of absolute poverty, study, preaching, and prayer.

But all these efforts would have failed, had not God prepared the souls of true mystics, apostolic souls wide open to the influence of His divine Spirit, and willing to receive in all its fullness the torrent of the fire of His love, and pour out that fire upon the world of heresy. God willed that the false mysticism of the Cathari should be devoured and destroyed by the purifying flames of divine love enkindled by Dominican, Franciscan, and Cistercian Saints. Perhaps the desire to pray and sacrifice herself more perfectly as a victim of reparation for the Catharist heresy had already had something to do with St. Lutgarde's entrance into Aywières, but in any case this motive began to exercise a powerful influence on her mystical vocation after her profession as a Cistercian.

It was through the Mother of God that her special vocation as victim for the heretics was announced to her.

The Blessed Virgin Mary appeared to St. Lutgarde with a face darkened with anguish, and the sight of our Lady's sorrow pierced the nun so deeply that she cried out: "What ails thee, O my dearest Lady, that thy face should be so haggard and so pale, thou, who art full of grace?"

The sorrowful Virgin replied: "Behold, my Son is once again being crucified by heretics and bad Christians. Once again they are spitting in His face. Do thou, therefore, do penance, and fast seven years, and appease the anger of my Son which now hangs heavy over the whole earth!"

The vision was gone, and Lutgarde, her heart on fire with desire to do penance for a world full of sin, began the first of her three seven-year fasts.

During these years she lived on nothing but bread and the ordinary drink of the convent, which happened to be weak beer. Fasts as extraordinary as this had been known in the Church before St. Lutgarde, and, indeed, the common fare of the old Fathers of the Desert had been little better than this and it is not usually claimed that their fasts were miraculous. In the case of a woman — and one of none too strong a constitution — such a feat was evidently much more surprising, and, to dispel every doubt as to its miraculous character, God presented evidence of it in the following sign.

St. Lutgarde was more than once ordered, under obedience, to take other food besides bread, but it was physically impossible for her to swallow anything else, "even a bean"[5] as her biographer tells us. Indeed, he adds that her fasts, instead of weakening her health, only increased her strength and her power of resistance.

This first seven-year fast was to be followed by another, and then a third, which only differed from it in minor details. The second was also the result of a revelation, and its intention, instead of being for "bad Christians and heretics" was for sinners at large. In addition to bread she put some vegetables on her diet this time.

[5] Nihil horum ad magnitudinem fabae guttur ejus transire praevaluit (*Vita*, 196 f).

St. Lutgarde had the character of her vocation more and more deeply impressed upon her soul by a series of visions during the time of this fast, visions which occurred almost daily, and usually took place at Mass. She would see Jesus standing before the face of His heavenly Father, showing Him His wounds, which had the appearance of having been freshly opened and were full of blood. Turning to Lutgarde, our Lord would say: "Do you not see how I offer Myself entirely to My Father, for My sinners? In the same way, I would have you offer yourself entirely to Me for My sinners, and avert the anger which has been kindled against them, in retribution for sin."

"*My* sinners": the phrase is twice repeated, in the narrative of Thomas of Cantimpré, and one feels that the saint had left her biographer with a deep awareness of its significance — an awareness which she had received directly from the lips of Christ in her vision. It is truly the voice of Christ's love that we hear speaking: the love that drove Him to the Cross to save sinners, to ransom all men from hell. Sinners belong to the infinite love who created them and sustains them every moment in being. But they belong by a special title to Jesus, to His Sacred Heart: for by dying for them, nailed to the Cross, He gained possession of them as His own.

The mystics of the Sacred Heart realized better than any others the intense urgency with which that love continually impels the glorified humanity of Christ to plead for *His* sinners in heaven.

But, what is more, the pleadings of the Sacred Heart are echoed and repeated throughout the Mystical Body that lives by the life of that Heart, by the charity which is His Holy Spirit.

When one member of a body suffers, all the others suffer with it. Christ can speak of *His* sinners just as truly as of His bleeding hands and feet: they are just as really part of Him, of His Mystical Body. They are its wounded members: perhaps they will have to be cut off, to save the other members that are still whole: but meanwhile, the healthy members plead for them, and join their prayers and tears to those of Christ, their Head, and of the Holy Ghost, their Heart.

And that was what St. Lutgarde, and so many others, once did on earth and do in heaven.

Her third seven-year fast brought her to the end of her life. Its intention was more specific and more urgent than either of the others. In 1239 or 1240, Christ again appeared to her, and warned her that His Church was exposed to attack by a powerful enemy. This attack would result in terrible harm to souls, unless someone undertook to suffer and win grace from God. Thus St. Lutgarde began her third and last fast. She was to die in its seventh year: but her death would be serene with the confidence of victory. Even in the year that preceded it, she was to tell Thomas of Cantimpré: "Dear friend, do not worry: this man who secretly desires the overthrow of the Church is either going to be humbled by the prayers of the faithful, or else he will soon depart this life, and leave the Church in peace."[6]

At the time when Thomas was writing, however, these prophecies had not yet been fulfilled, although they soon were to be, and so he did not venture to name the enemy who was most probably the Emperor Frederick II.

Frederick II, cultured and skeptical, devoured with pride and ambition and given to a life of indulgence, scarcely concealed his contempt for the Church and for the Christian religion — indeed, for all religion, and for the very notion of God. He had been heard to say that "three impostors, Christ, Moses, and Mohammed had led the world to its ruin." Presumably men like himself were destined to build it up, again

[6] *Vita*, 205 c.

by unbelief, debauchery, and war. It was also said of him that once, on seeing a priest carrying the Blessed Sacrament to a sick person, he had exclaimed: "How much longer will this comedy last?"[7]

He had found a determined and powerful opponent in the aged Pope Gregory IX, and the struggle had reached a crucial point about the time when St. Lutgarde began her third fast. The Pope had been unable to persuade St. Louis of France to take the field against the Emperor, because Louis refused to violate the treaties made with the Emperor by his father — a thing which was very fortunate for Frederick II, and which the latter probably secretly derided as a weakness. He himself, of course, was notorious for his disregard of treaties and agreements which did not suit his convenience.

In 1242 the Pope convoked a general council with intentions which Frederick had every reason to fear. So he had his soldiers in Piedmont, Liguria, and the Alps arrest all bishops and prelates passing into Italy from France to attend the council. A group of Cistercian abbots, including Bl. William, ex-abbot of Villers, and abbot of Clairvaux, were intercepted at sea by Frederick's agents, and thrown into prison. Bl. William died as a result of this confinement.[8]

At the time of St. Lutgarde's death, the Church was, so far as anyone could tell by natural means, still in grave danger from the Emperor. But soon afterward her prophecies were both fulfilled. Frederick II was first deposed, and then died suddenly in 1250, at the age of fifty-six.

In telescoping St. Lutgarde's three long fasts we have anticipated the course of our narrative, and given the reader a broad general view of her career as a Cistercian. We need only fill in the picture with a brief review of many other

[7] Mourret-Thompson, *History of the Church*, vol. iv, p. 591.
[8] His death crowned a long and holy life of service to the Church and the Order, which earned him veneration by the faithful. He is commemorated in the Cistercian Menology, May 24.

sufferings, interior and exterior, the chief of which was the
blindness which was added to her afflictions in the last
years of her life, and which will be discussed in its proper
place.

We have said that when the saint fled from St. Catherine's
to Aywières, she was trying not only to find a stricter, more
penitential, and more solitary life, but also to escape the
burden of her superiorship.

The fact that she was a stranger in Brabant, and could not
at first speak French, would not of itself have sufficed to
protect her from the same responsibilities either at Aywières
or at some other Cistercian convent among the French-speak-
ing Walloons. Indeed, when her reputation began to spread
beyond the enclosure walls of her new home, several new
foundations sought her as their prioress provided she would
learn French.

It would be underestimating and misunderstanding the
true simplicity and artlessness of Lutgarde, if we were to
assume that she deliberately refused to learn French to avoid
this responsibility. Thomas of Cantimpré represents her to
us as flying to the feet of the Blessed Virgin, and imploring
her aid, lest she come by any chance into possession of some
knowledge of the French tongue, or at least that variety of
the *Langue d'oil* that was spoken in West Flanders. Our
Lady reassured her in a vision and St. Lutgarde was never
able to her dying day to speak a word of French — at least
not in the ordinary course of events.

We can see the wisdom in the divine choice that brought
St. Lutgarde to Aywières rather than Herkenrode, where she
would never have been able to avoid some position of responsibility. God clearly destined her to remain in obscurity
and devote her whole life directly to Him alone in contemplation and penance. This is a favor which He by no means
reserves for all His chosen souls in the contemplative life:

often it is the ones most attracted to prayer and contemplation
that He draws out into the semiactive life of administration
in the spiritual or even temporal affairs of the monastery. The
resulting interior conflict is very purifying, and sometimes
leads rapidly and efficaciously to sanctity.

But St. Lutgarde was not destined to tread the ordinary
way.

The fear that she might perhaps learn French and be
chosen as superioress of some house was an insignificant thing
compared to certain other interior misgivings, mostly about
her prayer and the state of her own soul, which tormented
her at the beginning of her career at Aywières.

The chief of these was a scruple about distractions during
the Divine Office. In her intense fervor, Lutgarde fell a
prey to one of the subtle, but by no means unusual temptations, in which the evil spirit disguises himself as an angel
of light in order to warp and twist pure consciences. All
scruples have something of this character, and the choir of a
contemplative convent is a fertile breeding ground for them.

St. Lutgarde began to consider what attention she was
giving to the Office and came to the conclusion that she was
obliged to get through the hours without ever averting her
mind from her prayer, whether willingly or unwillingly, and
no matter whether the thought that came to her was holy or
unholy. She simply determined that she was going to think of
nothing but the words of the psalms, and what they signified,
and of God in whose presence she stood. Nothing else. Of
course, she soon discovered that this was impossible. At the
same time, she jumped to the conclusion that her distractions
made her Office worthless. Soon she was saying most of her
Office two or three times every day. There is probably almost
as much glee in hell over this sort of thing as there is over a
grave sin, simply because of the sad consequences to which
it can lead.

Evidently her sisters did not know much better than she did, for when she complained of her trouble, everybody took her seriously, and all prayed for her to get rid of her distractions. But God had mercy on her, and for our benefit as well as hers, got her out of her trouble by a supernatural revelation that her prayers were completely pleasing to Him because of her good will, and that, so far as their defects were concerned, He made up for them all with His own love and merits.[9]

Two things are to be noticed: first that our Lord, in His revelation, told St. Lutgarde that her recital of the Office was pleasing to Him, and second that it was nevertheless defective. Of course, the only defect of which there is question here is the inevitable wandering of the mind due to human weakness. The only conclusion is, then, that since even involuntary distractions are in some measure a defect in our Office, and since these defects are unavoidable, God desires in His mercy to make up for them Himself. However, there is a condition attached to this. We must, at least implicitly, acknowledge the defect as ours, and ask for His help and His forgiveness. Once we do this, we can gain much fruit from these little failures of ours. A patient and humble struggle to keep recollected will redound far more to our spiritual profit than would the ability to go through the entire Office without a distraction of any kind, as St. Lutgarde thought she was obliged to do.

It is consoling to learn that even the greatest mystics are purified by much the same trials and anxieties and temptations and perplexities as ordinary monks and nuns: but it should be more than merely consoling. Ought we not perhaps to conclude that if God tries us in the same fire, it is because

---

[9] Nullo ulterius pro dicendis horis dolore torquearis aut scrupulo: placabiles sunt orationes tuae et in conspectu meo gratanter acceptae. . . . Nihil verearis amplius, quoniam in te istum supplebo defectum (*Vita*, II, 199 f).

He would like to bring us to the same purity, and give us the same rewards? Surely that is not altogether unlikely: and if we do not make more progress, perhaps the reason is to be sought in the fact that we are not as generous as the great saints in our acceptance of these trials. We fail to recognize them as graces, we rebel against them, or allow ourselves to become discouraged and finally give up the struggle.[10]

[10] Cf. St. John of the Cross, *Living Flame of Love*, Stanza II, verse 5.

CHAPTER FOUR

THE SOULS IN PURGATORY. HER POWER OVER DEMONS. HER POWER OF HEALING

WE SOMETIMES hear of the ordinary trials of pious men and women — dryness in prayer, aridity and coldness of the will — spoken of as the "dark night of the soul." That is a misuse of the term. These sufferings are sometimes so natural and even so physical in their causes, that they cannot even be dignified by the title of "dark night of the senses." We must not immediately ascribe every fit of depression and despondency, and every passing shadow in the imagination and feelings, to the "dark night."

In the same way, it is often difficult to judge, from a few words in the narrative of a medieval author, whether the subject of his biography was undergoing the most extreme form of mystical purification, or simply the more ordinary kind of trial by the fire that spares the deeper faculties of the soul and confines its work to the interior senses and the sense appetite.[1]

When Thomas of Cantimpré tells us that St. Lutgarde was cast adrift on a wild, black sea of doubts and misgivings, and was tempted to fear that God had abandoned her and that her soul was lost, we are not entitled, on those grounds alone,

[1] It may be said that the Night of the Senses only attacks the intellect and will indirectly, through the senses and sense appetite. The Dark Night of the Soul is infinitely more terrible, since it strikes at the soul *from within itself,* and there is no means of knowing whence this persecution comes, or what it is.

to assert that she had entered into the dark night of the soul. The same doubts and misgivings might occur, and indeed often do occur, in the night of the senses — in which case, their seat is mostly in the imagination, and their chief effect is the ordinary passion of discouragement, with all its attendant circumstances and repercussions in the nervous system — lassitude, depression, and so on.

On the other hand, perhaps the best idea of the dark night of the soul, outside of St. John of the Cross's classical treatise, in which the term was invented, is to be found in the inspired words of the book of Job, in Jeremias, in some of the Psalms and in many other passages of Sacred Scripture — passages, however, which are obscure and full of difficulty.

Job, bound hand and foot in this terrible night, cried out: "I am brought to nothing: as a wind thou [God] hast taken away my desire, and my prosperity hath passed away like a cloud. . . . In the night my bone is pierced with sorrows: and they that feed upon me do not sleep. . . . I cry to thee and thou hearest me not: I stand up, and thou dost not regard me. . . . Thou hast lifted me up, and set me, as it were, upon the wind, and thou hast mightily dashed me."[2]

The Lamentations of Jeremias the Prophet paint the horror of this spiritual night in terms that make it sound like the experience of one buried alive: a soul in this state is as utterly abject and forsaken as a man bound hand and foot and laid in a sealed tomb. If anything, the feelings of the man buried alive would seem to be less terrifying: such a one could still have access to God in prayer. But the soul in the dark night feels as if God were the author of this persecution (as indeed He is) and begins to taste the cold terror of utter damnation, not realizing that this darkness is the ultimate purification worked by God's special love. Jeremias cries: "He hath built round about me, and he hath compassed me with

[2] Job 30:15, 17, 20, 22.

gall and labor. He hath set me in dark places, as those that are dead forever. He hath built against me round about, that I may not get out: he hath made my fetters heavy. Yea, and when I cry and entreat, he hath shut out my prayer. He hath shut up my way with square stones, he hath turned my paths upside down."[3]

Not content with this, the infinite purity of God attacks the soul with the blinding pain of His immediate presence — which causes fierce torture to the soul full of impurities and imperfections. In this way, God is ruthlessly burning out every stain, every slightest blemish in the soul: but the helpless and blinded victim sees nothing but the horror of its imperfections, and feels nothing but the furious attack of this force which it has no means of identifying or comprehending, except to know that it comes from God's infinite justice. So Jeremias continues: "He is become to me as a bear lying in wait: as a lion in secret places. He hath turned aside my paths, and hath broken me in pieces, and hath made me desolate. He hath bent his bow and set me as a mark for his arrows. He hath shot into my reins the daughters of his quiver."[3]

Jonas in the belly of the whale is another type of this almost unbearable desolation, and Christ Himself, in Gethsemani and in the final moments on the Cross drank this bitter chalice to its last black dregs. It was only because He did so that the prophets and the great saints were able to receive from God the special strength which alone would enable them to pass through this purgatorial fire without having their soul instantly torn from the body by the unspeakable anguish of the experience.

All that Thomas of Cantimpré tells us of St. Lutgarde's trial is contained in a few lines. The Holy Ghost overwhelmed her, as it were, in a stormy sea of anguish in which

---

[3] Lam. 3:5–13. Cf. also Jonas 2; Psalm 17, Psalm 87, etc., and St. John of the Cross, *Dark Night of the Soul*, Bk. ii, 2 and 3.

she was suddenly made aware of the nothingness of all her works and virtues — at least of her own part in them — and began to beg God for some assurance that she was not altogether lost.[4]

We can at least say that Thomas of Cantimpré is well within the traditional language and context of the dark night here, and of course St. Lutgarde's advanced spirituality and her mature mystical life would certainly lead one to expect this most arduous and rare of purifications at this point in her career. These interior trials do not, however, play a dominant part in her life: they are compensated for, as the reader will soon discover, by extraordinary bodily sufferings. No doubt, too, we must assume that these were always to some extent accompanied by a proportionate degree of interior desolation.

In any case, this particular trial came to an end with a revelation, or, to be precise, an interior locution, one detail of which is rather amusing. Lutgarde heard a voice assuring her that her life was pleasing to God. Momentarily comforted, she nevertheless became uneasy once more, after a brief interval of time. Then the divine voice again spoke within her.

"Would you like to have Mother Mary de Roavia bear witness to the security of your state?" In other words: "Would you like to have Me assure you that you are pleasing to Me, by sending you this nun to tell you so?"

Whoever Mother Mary de Roavia may have been, Lutgarde did not want her as a messenger. She cried out:

"O no, do not send *her*. She is far too timid. She would wait around for ages trying to make up her mind to come and tell me about it!"

Our Lord told her to set her mind at rest. He would send

---

[4] Spiritu quoque timoris Domini pia Lutgardis humiliter insignita, quasi tumentes fluctus, super se Dominum metuebat, et omnia opera sua, velut facta in dubio, verebatur (*Vita*, 197 c).

her someone else. And, as a matter of fact, four days later a stranger came to the convent and told Lutgarde, in the presence of most of the other nuns, that God was pleased with the state of her soul, and had, indeed, sent him there for the sole purpose of telling her so.

If St. Lutgarde suffered the anguish and desolation of purgatory while she was still on earth, it seems to have made her especially fervent in praying for the souls who were actually tormented in its flames. God, in His turn, was pleased to give her prayers for them a special efficacy.

Several visions and revelations granted to her in this connection are interesting not only in themselves, but also for the insight they give us into the history of the period.

The first of these visions has been regarded by some as a manifest delusion. It concerned one of the greatest of popes: Innocent III. Although he was not exactly regarded as a saint, the admiration of his contemporaries made it difficult for many to believe that he could have much to fear from purgatory. However, the learned annotator of the *Vita* in the Bollandists reminds us that the judgments of God are very different from those of men.[5]

In any case, in July, 1216, after the close of the Lateran Council (incidentally, it was the one which had given its approval to the projects which were soon to bear fruit in the organization of St. Dominic's Order of Preachers) St. Lutgarde suddenly saw the Sovereign Pontiff in a vision. His body was wrapped in a great flame. Lutgarde did not know the Pope had died — the news had not yet reached Belgium — and even if she had, she would not have been able to recognize him since she had never seen him.

"Who are you?" she asked of the figure in the flame.

"I am Pope Innocent."

"What," cried Lutgarde, overwhelmed with sorrow. "How

[5] *Vita,* 199 D, note e.

is it that you, our common father, are being tormented in such great pain?"

The Pope revealed to her three causes why he had rendered himself worthy even of hell, but said he had merited grace to escape that torment by founding a monastery dedicated to the Mother of God. Nevertheless, he said he had been consigned to purgatory until the Day of Judgment, but begged for her prayers — and added that the grace to appear to her and make known his great need had also been obtained for him by our Lady.

Lutgarde undertook some extraordinary penance for the soul of the great Pontiff, but its nature is not revealed to us by her biographer. Neither does he tell us the three causes of this suffering. Lutgarde had made them known to Thomas, but he decided to bury them in oblivion, out of respect for the memory of so eminent a Pope.

Eminent he had indeed been. His administrative and judicial genius had dominated his century, and his many other natural gifts and supernatural graces have always caused him to be the object of admiration to men. The fact that he had had to show himself extremely firm in defense of the Church against powerful temporal interests had, no doubt, aroused prejudices against him, and it is sometimes argued that perhaps some rumor, some echo of this enmity, had filtered into the convent and into the mind of St. Lutgarde, and influenced her, without her realizing it, in this vision. The mere fact that such a thing is not absolutely impossible is not enough to make us accept it as a valid supposition when the other mystical graces in her life are so well authenticated. On the other hand, of course, genuine mystics have been mistaken in particular cases. How are we to judge, on the basis of one rather summary biography, seven hundred years after the fact? We cannot.

A similar vision concerning Pope Innocent III was had

by Bl. Simon of Aulne, a contemporary of St. Lutgarde's, famous for his charismatic gifts, especially for his miraculous knowledge of the secrets of souls. This holy Cistercian lay brother had even been summoned to Rome by the same Innocent III, at the time of the Lateran Council, that is, shortly before his death, and the Pope had consulted him not only on matters of Church policy but even personal spiritual affairs.[6]

Closer to home, and more useful as a subject of meditation for Cistercians, was the case of a certain abbot who owed his liberation from purgatory to St. Lutgarde. This man, a learned and talented nobleman from Germany, entered the Cistercian Order and became abbot of Foigny.[7] A fervent lover of the Rule, he had nevertheless failed to grasp the tremendous importance of its seventy-third chapter, and St. Benedict's condemnation of that "evil zeal of bitterness which separates men from God and leads them into hell."

Simon (as the abbot was called) tried to enforce the Rule in the harsh, disciplinarian spirit of an army officer, instead of applying it with the wisdom and discretion of a loving father. He had the misfortune to die suddenly in this frame of mind, and soon found out how little there was of the spirit of Christ in his way of training men.

St. Lutgarde had known him before his entrance into the Order, and was greatly afflicted at the news of his death, so that she began to pray and do penance and fast, begging God most insistently for his release. Soon she received an answer,

---

[6] The thirteenth-century life of this saint, edited in the seventeenth century by one Moschus, a priest of Armentieres, is available in a French version in the work of P. Nimal, C.S.S.R., *Villers et Aulne*.

[7] Foigny was the third foundation made by St. Bernard as abbot of Clairvaux. It was situated in the diocese of Laon, France. The various manuscript readings of the name in the *Vita* make it doubtful whether or not Foigny is referred to here. However, the case is proved by *Gallia Christiana*. Cf. Jonquet, *Ste. Lutgarde, la Marguerite Marie Belge*, p. 153, n.

from the divine Voice, that her prayers were favorably received, and that all would be well with her friend. But
Lutgarde was not satisfied with so vague a statement. It was
not enough to know that he *might* get out of purgatory some
time soon, she wanted to hear that he was definitely in
heaven. Until then, she could not rest, and, returning to
the attack, she pleaded with the Sacred Heart to take away
whatever consolations He had destined for her, and to grant
them all to the poor suffering soul of the abbot of Foigny.

Christ did not keep her ardent charity any longer in
suspense. He presently appeared to her, and brought with
Him the soul for whom she had interceded with such loving
insistence.

"Dry your tears, My beloved," said our Lord to the saint.
"Here he is." Lutgarde flung herself face downward on the
floor, adoring the mercy of God and blessing Him for His
bounty. The soul of Abbot Simon, exulting and praising
God, thanked his benefactress, and she saw him pass on
into heaven.

We must not imagine that these visions of disembodied
souls passed before the mind (perhaps even the bodily eyes)
of St. Lutgarde without striking her to the depth of her soul
with movements of wonder, love, and fear. Perhaps the most
terrifying experience was that by which she was supernaturally
informed of the death of her own sister. Suddenly, one day,
in the air above her head, she heard a terrible, resounding cry,
the voice of a woman in great anguish: "Have mercy on me,
dearest sister! have mercy on me and pray for me, and obtain
mercy for me, as you did for all those other souls!" Soon afterward, the news of her sister's death reached her by ordinary
means, confirming what she had heard.

Then there was the holy priest Jean de Lierre, on whose
advice she had entered Aywières. He did not have to appeal
to her from purgatory. These two saintly souls had made

a pact with one another, in which they mutually promised that the first of them to die would appear to the other and make the fact known. It is not the kind of an agreement that can be entered into by just anyone, in a casual sort of way, nor would we recommend this sort of thing to the interest and concern of those who desire to progress in a life of prayer and union with God. After all, the important thing is union with God, and not conversations with souls in purgatory or even in heaven. Nevertheless, where the mysterious designs of God have decreed that there be some utility in such things, in a particular case like that of St. Lutgarde, they are worthy of consideration, though not of imitation.

Jean de Lierre, in any case, had gone to Rome on a mission in behalf of some convents under his direction in the Low Countries, and died while crossing the Alps. He did not delay in keeping his bargain, but appeared to Lutgarde in the cloister at Aywières. The fact that she was not surprised to see him there and that, believing him to be alive, she made him a sign to step into the parlor, presents a problem which we cannot delay to try and solve here. But we can at least face the dilemma: either Thomas of Cantimpré's words *"in claustri ambitu"* do not have reference to the cloister, or else Aywières was not as strict about enclosure as Cistercian convents at the time generally were. *Claustrum* might conceivably mean "enclosure" and *ambitus* might refer to a path around the outside of the enclosure wall. On the other hand, perhaps Jean de Lierre, as a priest and director of souls might have had some official reason that would account for his presence in the cloister of the Cistercian nuns of Aywières.

In any case, St. Lutgarde saw Jean de Lierre inside or outside the convent, somewhere near the door to the parlor where the nuns were permitted to speak to visitors, and she made him a sign to go in. He replied to her, saying:

"I am dead. I have left this world. But I have come to

keep my bargain with you, and inform you of my death as I promised before God."

Falling on her knees before him Lutgarde suddenly saw his garments filled with splendor, blazing in white and red and blue. Asking him the meaning of these colors she was told that the white signified the spotless innocence of virginity which the saintly man had preserved all his life, the red betokened the labors and sufferings in the cause of justice which had absorbed so much of his time and energy during life and which had eventually led to his death. The blue showed the perfection of his spiritual life — a term by which Thomas probably means his life of prayer, his union with God.

Another director of souls — a religious, who had been confessor to the nuns at Aywières — did not merit this blue garment. Fr. Baldwin of Barbenzon was not a Cistercian, for he became prior of the Canons Regular at Oignies, where Bl. Mary of Oignies, St. Lutgarde's spiritual friend, had been venerated since her death in 1213.

Bl. Mary had probably been brought into contact with Lutgarde by Jacques de Vitry, her biographer, and she had paid high tribute to Lutgarde's sanctity. Bl. Mary exclaimed on her deathbed: "There is no one on this earth more faithful to the Lord than Mother Lutgarde, and no one whose prayers are more powerful in liberating souls from purgatory: nor is there any one more mighty here below, in obtaining grace for sinners."[8]

Baldwin of Barbenzon, with whom we are concerned, made the mistake of letting himself get too involved in worldly business. Engrossed in temporal matters, the character of

[8] Sub coelo non habet mundus Domina Lutgarde fideliorem, et magis efficacem in precibus pro liberandis animabus a purgatorio, et pro peccatoribus exoratricem (*Vita*, 198 b). Jacques de Vitry's life of St. Mary of Oignies is translated in Fr. Nimal's collection: "*Les Grandes Saintes du Pays de Liège*," Liège, 1898. Cf. *Acta Sanctorum*, Jun., V, 545.

which was, apparently, none too clean, he was suddenly overtaken by a mortal illness, and within a short time found himself in the cold portals of death. As the door was about to close upon him, he begged for a relic of the holy recluse, Bl. Mary, to be brought to him, and implored her with the greatest earnestness to obtain mercy for him.

Then he died and was buried. St. Lutgarde's confessor at this time was the Dominican, Fra Bernard, and he had attended the funeral of the prior of Oignies. Returning to Aywières, he was met by Lutgarde, who said:

"So Fr. Baldwin is dead!"

"Dead and buried," said the astonished priest, and asked his penitent how on earth she came to know about it. She told him that Bl. Mary of Oignies had appeared to her and urged her to rise up in haste and pray earnestly for their mutual friend, who was even then appearing before the judgment seat of God, to give an account of "all his omissions and all his commissions."

Just what these may have been, we are not told, and we need not inquire. It is evident, reading between the lines of Thomas of Cantimpré, that he had allowed his fervor to cool and had turned into one of those worldly clerics, interested more in money and in good food and their own solid comfort than in the service of God and of souls. "Behold," he says, "with how severe a judgment are they judged who, according to the word of Isaias, beat the sword of the word of God into the plowshares of temporal business; and cast aside the spears of invective against sin, in order to reap a harvest of delights and taste the fruits of a peace that must inevitably pass from them with time."[9]

And now, an interesting and difficult question is raised by these visions. What exactly was it that St. Lutgarde *saw*? In two cases she saw a "spirit," one in the flames of purgatory,

[9] *Vita*, 206 b.

one on the way to glory. Then, she heard a voice. We do not know what it was she saw when Mary of Oignies appeared to her: but perhaps it was a vision of the saint as she had been in her lifetime. Finally, when she first saw Jean de Lierre, he seemed to be an ordinary living man. Setting aside the case of the voice, for the time being, let us briefly consider these visions.

The problem is twofold: it is generally agreed by mystical theologians that the essential vision of an angelic spirit or of a disembodied soul is not for this life.[10]

But, on the other hand, the souls in purgatory and the saints in glory have no bodies. When, therefore, they appear *with* bodies, are these bodies objectively real, and if so where do they come from? Or is the vision of them only subjective?

When St. Lutgarde saw John de Lierre, she believed she was seeing a living man in the ordinary way. This was a corporeal, or bodily vision: one which is, in itself, the least perfect kind of mystical vision granted to men on earth, although it does possess a certain perfection in the sense that it is most strictly connatural to us — it is most suited to our ordinary way of seeing.

Theologians have entered into some rather fantastic discussions of these "bodies" that appear to the saints in visions. There is a general agreement that such bodies can have an objective and physical reality. St. Thomas, speaking of miraculous appearances of Christ in the Blessed Sacrament, for instance in the form of a Child, or crowned with thorns, as He had appeared before the faithful at Herkenrode, expresses the opinion that when these visions appear to many people at the same time, and last for a long time, they are probably caused by an objective and real species, miraculously present, though not the actual glorified body of Christ. But when only one person sees them, he thinks it is safer to

[10] Cf. St. John of the Cross, *Ascent of Mount Carmel*, ii, ch. 22.

hold that the species is caused by God, subjectively, in the eye of the beholder.[11]

The discussion degenerates, under the tender mercies of minor theologians, into futile speculations as to whether the bodies of saints, appearing in these visions, are formed by the work of angels, and if so, what they are made of. "Very refined" atoms? Compressed air? Rays of light? And so on. It is significant that when the great mystical theologian, St. John of the Cross, comes to talk about corporal visions he does not even bother with such trifling questions: he simply tells us that these visions are of little importance anyway, and that we should simply ignore them and pay no attention to them whatever. Thus we will avoid the deceptions of the devil and of our own imagination, while, if they *do* happen to come from God, their good effect will not be impeded by our resistance to mere external curiosities.[12] As to what kind of atoms the angels use in building up these "bodies," or whether the bodies are objective or subjective, St. John does not bother to inquire.

We now have two alternatives: either a visible body is formed outside the beholder in space, or the species, the image of a body is formed in the eye of the one seeing the vision. There is another possibility. St. Lutgarde might have had an *imaginary* vision, in which God caused the species to be formed directly in the imagination, without any activity on the part of the exterior senses. Her visions of the souls of Pope Innocent and of Simon the Abbot of Foigny might have come under this category, and probably that of John de Lierre did also. But it is possible that when St. Lutgarde saw the two disembodied souls, and our Lord, and St. Mary of Oignies, she was having *spiritual* visions. In this case, her intellect would have been directly illuminated by the divine light, and she

[11] St. Thomas, III, q. lxxvi, a. 8.
[12] *Ascent of Mount Carmel*, ii, ch. 10.

would have seen the souls in something approaching the essential vision that will be given to us by the light of glory. Spiritual, or intellectual visions reveal to the soul, in a sudden blazing intuition, the intimate nature of things or persons. They are not only far more perfect, in themselves, than imaginary or corporeal visions, but they are elevated beyond the sphere in which the devil or our own lower nature can enter in to deceive us. On the other hand, we must not suppose that because they are most perfect *in themselves,* they necessarily make a *greater impression* on individual men and women. In an exceptionally purified soul, they will, no doubt, also have a greater effect: but ordinarily the imaginary visions are those which make the strongest appeal to our nature, in its mixture of rationality and sensibility: for much more striking effects can be produced in the imagination than in the intellect. This is why the devil, as St. John of the Cross points out, prefers the imagination before all other domains, as a sphere of activity in deluding souls.[18]

Therefore, to conclude this digression, while we may admire the work performed by God in the soul of the saint through the means of these visions we need not envy her, nor try to emulate her in them. Our efforts would be useless in any case: these things are entirely beyond our powers. Instead of courting the unwelcome assistance of the devil by desiring them, we will do better to concentrate on uniting ourselves to God by perfect faith and pure love. In this, St. Lutgarde's example is far more valuable. For, after all, these visions were absolutely without merit, in themselves. It was her ardent charity, her

[18] The sense of imagination and phantasy is the devil's favorite domain. It lends itself so well to his machinations, both natural and preternatural. It is the front door to the soul, a kind of harbor-landing, or market place where the understanding comes to shop for whatever it likes . . . (from the French edn. of Canon Hoornaert). *Ascent of Mount Carmel,* ii, ch. 14 (vol. i, p. 120). For spiritual visions, see the same work, ii, ch. 22 (*ibid.,* p. 173).

fervent and persistent patience in praying for souls, and in beleaguering the gates of heaven with penance and fasting and supplication for their benefit, that filled her soul with grace and united her more and more closely to God with each new aspiration and prayer for the members of His Church Suffering.

Wherever the Holy Spirit works in souls with His seven gifts and *gratiae gratis datae* to produce the superabundance of mystical life, as He was doing among contemplative religious and recluses, as well as holy persons in the world in the Low Countries during St. Lutgarde's lifetime, the devil tries to frustrate that work by turning the love of God into love of mysticism for its own sake. It is hard, even for the most sincere and vigilant, to resist the subtle tendency of self-love to appropriate everything to itself; prayer can so easily become an earnest and presumptuous quest for whatever makes us appear great in our own estimation and in that of men.

There was a nun in Aywières who had allowed herself to be deluded by the dark angel, and was walking the paths of false mysticism, under his adroit and flattering guidance. St. Lutgarde was praying for her one day, when she heard the divine voice. God said to her: *"Illuminare his qui in tenebris et in umbra mortis sedent."* Lutgarde was familiar enough with the Latin words, but did not know their meaning, although she recited them at least twice on most days of the year (three times, if the nuns recited the Little Office). She had to inquire from one of the other nuns to discover that they meant: "To enlighten them that sit in darkness and in the shadow of death."[14]

Even this did not make it absolutely clear what she was to do, but she returned to her prayers with renewed fervor. Then, suddenly, a devil appeared to her, and declared: "I am

---

[14] From the Canticle of Zachary: *Benedictus*, Luke 1:79.

the lying spirit who deceive that nun." Lutgarde was not accepting any statements from a devil, not even if he happened to confess that he was a liar! Besides, a lying spirit might well choose an announcement of that fact as a new and subtle means of perpetrating some deception. However, she was not afraid of him, and she seems to have been serenely confident of a special power to command obedience from him, implicit in the very fact of his self-revelation, which, if it were true, was only to be attributed to direct compulsion from God. So she said to the devil: "Go to Brother Simon, at the monastery of Aulne, and tell him what you have just told me, and we will see if he bears witness to the truth of what you say." This was the same Brother Simon who had been called to Rome by Innocent III, because of his fame as a prophet. He was a man, says Thomas of Cantimpré, full of the Spirit of God and one to whom God had revealed many things. His reputation as a seer won him rather easy and frequent permissions to travel, which, incidentally, he did not consider much of a favor as he would have preferred to have been left in peace at the little isolated grange where he was appointed to take care of the sheep.

However, he soon put in an appearance at Aywières and confirmed what Lutgarde had been told. They decided to confront the deluded nun and her devil, and see what could be done about them.

The nun was brought into the room where St. Lutgarde and Bl. Simon and several others were gathered. As soon as the false mystic came into their presence, she was seized with a sudden rigor, as though she were dead. Her limbs became as rigid as wood. She looked as if she had been instantaneously and completely frozen, and her mouth was shut so tight that it could not even be pried open with a knife. Her devil wanted to be sure that she did not answer any questions. The sight was so appalling that it was enough to strike every heart cold with fear, and all who were in the room fell to their knees and began to beseech God to help the unfortunate sister.

Incidents like this are frequent in the lives of saints: we read of them in their bare outline. We become a little accustomed to the theme, and lose the sense of the horrifying reality of the spirits of darkness and their work. We are all too ready to take for granted the special protection of God which keeps the mighty malignity of these hellish powers from pouring out their hate upon our souls and bodies according to the measure of their desires.

The power of the devil was not able to resist the strength of the prayers that were poured out before God on that day. The body of the unfortunate nun relaxed, and her limbs came back to life, she was able to open her mouth and to take a little food. From that time on she was delivered from the spirit of deception.

Since she was after all a sincere and worthy religious, she rather profited by the experience. It must have taught her plenty of humility and prudence. Thomas of Cantimpré knew her well, and testifies that she became an exemplary nun, not only herself enlightened in the darkness in which she had once walked, but a light to many others as well.[15]

Another Cistercian nun, her convent is not mentioned, suffered for many years from furious temptations of the flesh. She was, herself, a most chaste and innocent virgin, and Thomas of Cantimpré can only ascribe the strength of these temptations to the fact that a devil must have been given special power to torment her body, and to subject her to such violence as almost to deprive her of her reason. At times it almost seemed that the evil one was about to hurl her bodily out the doors of the convent and drive her headlong into sin.

---

[15] *Vita*, Lib. iii, no. 8, 197–198. This incident is also related in the ms. life of Bl. Simon, cf. *Vita*, 199, n. g.

We may take Thomas' word, concerning the cause of these paroxysms: but at the same time, we must remember that certain characters allow their imagination and emotions to become so upset by the ordinary movements of the flesh, that they cause a normal and natural physical phenomenon to become exaggerated into a tempest of the spirit. They do themselves much harm, and produce a state of nervous excitement which the devil might well exploit for his own sinister ends.

Whatever was behind these temptations, the nun was entirely delivered from them by the prayers of St. Lutgarde, and never suffered from them again.

Lutgarde was moved with a special charity for the agonizing. She not only prayed for them in general, but she was especially zealous in visiting the dying in the convent infirmary, and giving them all the spiritual and material assistance at her command. The traditions of Catholic piety should keep us very much alive to the fact that, at the last hour of life, when we are physically and mentally helpless and practically unable to pray, we are badly in need of companionship and prayer: and then, most of all, does the devil seek to take advantage of our state, in a last, furious effort to possess the soul that he sees slipping out of his grasp forever.

Once, in the convent infirmary, a nun lay dying. As the agony began, the community arrived to say the regular prayers that accompany a dying Cistercian to the gate of death. Then St. Lutgarde saw the devil. He hastened by her, livid with rage. He explained, on his way out: "Lo, I was tormenting that nun! And then this mob arrived, and I was no longer able to do anything to her."

Frequently, says Thomas of Cantimpré,[16] summing up

16 *Vita,* 199 b.

St. Lutgarde's experiences with evil spirits, frequently the demons would come up to her and announce something woeful or gloomy. Upon which she would spit at them, or, if they became too much of a nuisance, she would drive them away with a sign of the cross. As a matter of fact, he adds, they were so afraid of her that they would no more go near the place where she prayed in church, than if it had been made of red-hot iron.

Although she did not understand Latin, nevertheless her most efficacious means of driving away the devil and his temptations was to turn over in her mind the lines of some Psalm, for instance, *Deus in adjutorium meum intende* (O God, come to my assistance). So strong was her faith in the power of even the material words of Divine Revelation, that she derived more benefit from Scripture than many an erudite, but less holy, theologian.

Bl. Mary of Oignies prophesied on her deathbed that Lutgarde would obtain from God many miraculous cures for the faithful, after passing from this life into heaven, saying that before that time she would also work many spiritual miracles.[17] That was true: but it was also true that even in this life, St. Lutgarde worked several actual miracles.

A woman had a son, a boy named John, who had epileptic fits. One night, in a dream, she heard the words: "Go to Mother Lutgarde, who lives at Aywières, and she will deliver your son from his sickness." Accordingly, the very next day the mother arose and took her child and went to Aywières. Lutgarde said a prayer, put her finger in his mouth, at the same time making a sign of the cross on his chest with her thumb, and from that day forth he was completely cured.

There was a nun at Aywières called Elizabeth — it would

[17] Spiritualia miracula in vita sua nunc facit; corporalia post mortem efficiet (*Vita*, 198 b).

be hard to say, exactly, whether it was the saintly Elizabeth de Wans to whom St. Lutgarde appeared after her death,[18] who had long been confined to the infirmary with a strange disease. All we know about it are two facts. First, she was so weak that if she got out of bed she immediately collapsed, and second, on account of this extreme weakness, she had to be fed at frequent intervals of the day and night if her strength was to be maintained at all.

One day St. Lutgarde who, with her seven-year fasts, was at the other extreme from this poor Elizabeth, had just received Communion, and was so overwhelmed with consolations that it was physically impossible for her to eat anything at all. It was a Sunday, and dinner immediately followed Sext and the major Conventual Mass, which was the one at which general Communion was given in the Middle Ages.[19]

One might have expected that Lutgarde would complain of the situation. She might, perhaps, have asked our Lord why the sisters had to go to dinner right after Sext, when they would have liked to prolong their thanksgiving and taste the delights of His company in the secrecy of their souls. Instead, she reproached Him for putting her at odds with the convent schedule with His untimely consolations. "Lord," she said, "this is not the proper time for me to have all this delight and sweetness. Why don't You go to Elizabeth who can hardly go for an hour without food, and take possession of her heart, and let me go and get something to eat, and build up my strength."

See, says Thomas of Cantimpré, what a wise woman Lut-

---

[18] Cf. *Vita*, 209 c. Elizabeth de Wans was accorded the title "Blessed" by the *Gazophylacium Belgicum*, according to a note in the Bollandists, *Vol. cit.*, 210, note e. See p. 143 ff., this present work.

[19] On feast days at the present time, all Cistercians who are not priests receive Communion, on days of two Masses, at the earlier Mass, usually the matutinal Mass (outside of Lent) which is said (not sung) before the morning Chapter, at about six o'clock. On ordinary days, Communion is distributed at the Mass *de Beata* or private Masses, about 4:30 a.m.

garde was![20] She was not the kind who, as soon as they get
a little consolation, forget all their obligations, and let everything go, health and all, in order to drink their sensible joy
to the last drop, and revel in their passing fervor while it
lasts. He is right: for, after all, St. Lutgarde could not be
accused of worrying too much about her health, when she
felt obliged to take the little food that was absolutely necessary
to hold body and soul together. After all, she subsisted for
twenty-one years of her life on a diet that might have killed
many stronger constitutions than hers in half that time. And
it is quite evident that in preferring God's signified will in this
clear duty to take at least the minimum care of her body she
was doing something far more pleasing to Him than her
prayers would have been. It is not by our feelings of fervor
that we please God, but by the sacrifice of our will. It is not
our sweet words that He wants, but our love, in deed and
in truth. Consequently, when St. Lutgarde sacrificed the
inebriating joys of a quasi-ecstatic union with the God who
is the very source of all life and all delight, in order to
perform a function which gave her very little pleasure, merely
to maintain, for His sake, the health of a body from which
she would have been glad to be separated, she offered Him a
most pleasing sacrifice.

The important thing is, however, that her prayer was
answered. She was set free, and the sufferer in the infirmary
was suddenly invaded with spiritual joys: and they were so
intense that, to the astonishment of her attendants, she not
only did not need any food but was unable to eat for some
time. How long this state of affairs lasted, we do not know.
But, eventually, through the prayers of St. Lutgarde, Sister
Elizabeth obtained the object of her ardent desire, which was
to be able to get out of bed and return to the ordinary community life, and keep the whole Rule like the other nuns.

[20] *Vita,* 200 b.

The next incident would have been somewhat irregular in a modern Cistercian convent, where it is forbidden to use the sign-language of the Order in church, except to prevent some confusion in the functions of the liturgy. The rules seem to have been less rigid at Aywièrcs in the thirteenth century.

There was a good lady of Liége called Matilda, who had two grown sons in the army and had lost her husband. Leaving what property she had to the two soldiers, she entered Aywières to finish her life peacefully in the service of God. She was getting to be an old lady, and was quite deaf.

One day, while the choir was singing Vespers of some great feast, someone made a sign to old Sister Matilda, to the effect that the nuns were singing very high and it was just beautiful to hear them. The poor old lady caught the meaning of the sign, and bowed her head and began to cry because she was so deaf that she had not heard a thing.

Lutgarde came in just then and saw her crying, and made her a sign, asking what was the matter. Sister Matilda replied that she was crying because she was deaf, and could not hear the singing. Thomas of Cantimpré does not say that she used signs, either. Sometimes old people in the Order, especially if they have been long in the infirmary where they talk to their attendants, get to the state where signs are hardly necessary any more — there is so much semi-deliberate whispering to accompany the movement of the fingers!

The saint was sorry for the poor old sister. She knelt and prayed a little, then, rising, she moistened her fingers with saliva and placed them in Matilda's ears. And then the old nun suddenly felt the wall that barred all sound from her mind break down with a roar, and her ears being opened, she heard the sweet singing in a rush of clear and wonderful sound. And she began to magnify the power of God in His holy servant Lutgarde.

CHAPTER FIVE

SINNERS

ONE of the most beautiful of our Votive Masses is the Mass of Our Lord's Passion, in the Cistercian Missal. It is, in many respects, the same as the old Votive Mass of the Five Wounds, found in the Ancient Missal of the Order. Built upon the foundation of the deeply moving prophecy of the Passion in the twelfth chapter of Zacharias, and the words in which the Evangelist St. John describes with terrifying objectivity and restraint the death of the Man-God on the cross (which he himself witnessed) this Mass is one of the most impressive and powerful liturgical monuments of the high Middle Ages.

"And I will pour out upon the House of David and upon the inhabitants of Jerusalem the spirit of grace and of prayers," cries the voice of the Spirit in the words of His prophet Zacharias, in the Epistle of this Mass. "And they shall look upon He whom they have pierced: and they shall mourn for Him as one mourneth for an only son, and they shall grieve over Him as the manner is to grieve for the death of the first-born. In that day, there shall be a great lamentation in Jerusalem, . . . and they shall say to Him, what are these wounds in the midst of Thy hands? And He shall say, with these was I wounded in the house of them that loved Me. Awake, O sword, against My shepherd, and against the man that cleaveth to Me, saith the Lord of hosts; strike the shepherd and the sheep shall be scattered, saith the Lord almighty."[1]

"What are these wounds in the midst of Thy hands?" Lutgarde was to cry, in spirit, to her Christ, and all her years at Aywières were to be amazed and filled with sorrow at His reply: "With these was I wounded in the house of them that loved Me!"

It is not strange, indeed, that pagans and heathens and heretics in their ignorance should live in sins and die in them. Far more terrible is the perverse and sluggish coldness of those who have received the gift of faith and tasted the joy of being children of God, and who, nevertheless, are ready to throw away their inestimable heritage of peace in this life and beatitude in the next for a burden of intolerable cares in this life and damnation in the next. Devotion to Christ's merciful love for sinners turns first of all to the pierced Heart of the Saviour and to His wounded hands and feet. It turns to the Cross and the Eucharist, in a hopeless effort to comprehend such infinite depths of charity: but the abyss is too great for our minds. The contrast between God's love and man's stupidity and ingratitude is so far beyond our powers of mind to fathom and of will to repair by love, that the sheer effort to do something about it often baffles our whole spiritual vitality, drains us of all our power to act. There sometimes seems to be nothing for us to do but admit our helplessness, and look to Him in expectant silence, waiting in the darkness, trusting Him to enlighten us, and show us how we are to serve Him and make amends for sin. Indeed, reparation takes on a deeper meaning when we enter into this naked night of humiliation and powerlessness, by which our true relation to God, as creatures who have rebelled against their Creator, is brought home to us at last.

[1] This Epistle is a mosaic of passages from chapters twelve and thirteen of Zach. 12:10–11; 13:6, 7. This is the Epistle of the present Votive Mass of the Passion in the Cistercian Missal.

It is not enough to wonder at the love of Christ, pierced with nails and bleeding to death for us on the Cross. It is not enough to see and consider the Passion, or to be dismayed by the persistence and stubbornness of sin. We must taste and experience something of the Passion ourselves. We must share His Cross. We must feel the burning thirst that was in the body and in the soul of Christ on the Cross: His thirst for our souls, His thirst for the souls of all men. And we must share it by thirsting in charity for the perfect possession of Him, and for the salvation and glorification of all men. Christ looks down upon the world seeking souls who are willing, like St. Paul, to rejoice in sufferings for sinners, and to fill up those things that are wanting of the sufferings of Christ in their flesh, for His body, which is the Church.[2]

The Gospel of the old Votive Mass of the Five Wounds brings this all before us. "In those days, Jesus knowing that all things were now accomplished, that the Scripture might be fulfilled said: *I thirst.* Now there was a vessel set there, full of vinegar. And they, putting a sponge full of vinegar about hyssop, put it to His mouth. Jesus, therefore, when He had taken the vinegar said: It is consummated. And bowing His head, He gave up the ghost."

Then we are told how the Jews hastened to Pilate, to have the Body of Him whom they had pierced taken down from the Cross, and how the Roman soldier, scarcely able to believe that this Man was already dead, pierced His side, and "immediately there came out blood and water."[3]

Yet this Mass is not without its note of triumph. For this crucified Jesus is our King, and it is in His Cross alone that we glory: for if we accept with joy all sufferings and trials, it is not for their own sake but because of the love and glory

[2] Col. 1:24.
[3] John 19:28–35. It is practically the same as the Gospel for the Mass of the Sacred Heart.

which they enable us to give to our King. Even before they beheld Him dying, in this Gospel, on the Cross, the old Cistercians had sung, in the *Alleluia* verse: "Hail Thou our King! Thou alone hadst mercy upon our errors, and, obeying Thy Father, wast led to the Cross, as a meek lamb to the slaughter. Glory be to Thee, hosanna! Triumph and victory to Thee, and a crown of supernal praise!"[4]

Without attempting to prove that this Mass existed in the Cistercian missal in St. Lutgarde's time, we can point to it as an authentic manifestation of the spirituality of the Order even in days of St. Bernard, and the writings of the saint are enough to bear us out. But if the works of St. Bernard had all perished, the life of St. Lutgarde would serve us as a living embodiment of a spirituality whose very core was the pierced Heart of Christ, and whose supreme prayer was His "*Sitio.*" We need not use the historic tense. It is also the spirituality of the Cistercians of today.

So great was the ardor and intensity of the burning thirst that was Lutgarde's desire to be united with Christ, that she used to cry out to Him daily begging Him to send her death, that she might be delivered from darkness, and come to Him in the glorious light of heaven. We read of such desires in the saints: they are the work, not of their own efforts and striving, not of some intensified inner drive of the imagination and emotions toward God. They are produced by the Holy Spirit through infused love. It is not, therefore, something that anyone can set himself to imitate by acts of his own un-aided will. One may try, of course: and a rush of sentimental tears may reward the first earnest efforts. But that is not infused love. And the end of the whole business may perhaps be a general relapse into depression and physical lassitude.

[4] Ave Rex noster: tu solus nostros miseratus errores, Patri obediens, ductus es ad crucem ut agnus mansuetus ad occisionem. Tibi gloria, osanna, tibi triumphus et victoria, tibi supernae laudis corona.

When Christ heard St. Lutgarde crying out to Him, in the heat of this fierce spiritual thirst, He replied by reminding her of His own "*Sitio*." He appeared to her in a vision, and laying open to her eyes the wounds of His hands and feet and side, He gently reproved the selfishness of her desire by saying:

"See, My beloved, contemplate what My wounds cry out to thee, lest the shedding of My Blood be in vain, and lest My death be useless."

And when St. Lutgarde saw and heard this, her heart was moved with a great fear, and she trembled to the very depths of her being, so real and terrible a thing was it, to her, to understand that Christ was not altogether pleased with her request. And she begged Him, in anguish, to enlighten her, to tell her what it was that His wounds cried out to her.

"They tell thee," Christ replied, "to labor and to weep, for thy labors and tears will quench the enkindled anger of My Father, and will persuade Him not to hurl sinners down to their death, but to show them His mercy, that they may live."[5]

St. Teresa, in her "fifth mansion," explains how God works upon the soul that has been brought by His Spirit to mystical union, and purifies it from the imperfection of a more or less selfish desire for the joys of heaven, by leading it on to the higher and more perfect act of abandonment to His divine will in all things, whether life or death, suffering or joy, darkness or consolation.[6]

This is simply the third degree of the love of God given to us by St. Bernard in his "*De Diligendo Deo*," the degree in which we no longer love God for ourselves, but for *Himself*. To love God for Himself, however, means to love His will

---

[5] . . . Pia Lutgardis pavefacta mirifice, cum timore et horrore quaesivit; quis esset clamor vulnerum Christi? et responsum est ei: Labore tuo et fletibus, iram patris mitigabis accensam, ut non perdat peccatores in mortem, sed per misericordiam Dei convertantur et vivant (*Vita*, 197 d).

[6] St. Teresa, *The Interior Castle*, V, chap. 2, Stanbrook translation, p. 100.

simply because it is His will: to find all our joy in the accomplishment of His will. But if all our joy is that His will be done, then we will necessarily feel pain, at least on this earth, when His will is not done. We will necessarily suffer interiorly as Christ suffered in His Sacred Heart, at the sins committed against Him.

One important distinction must, however, be made. The soul that is so united to God as truly to suffer, on account of sin, as Christ suffered, will never feel any sense of outrage or indignation toward the person of a *sinner*. If he does, he may know, by this, that his union with the Sacred Heart is by no means perfect, and that imagination and passion play a large part in his sorrow.

The true sorrow, which gave the saints a taste of Christ's bitter chalice in Gethsemani, is a participation in the anguish of infinite love, seeking to give souls joy and peace and everlasting life, and yet rejected by them.

St. Teresa, then, speaking of this development in the mystical life of the soul, thinks that God gives this share in the sufferings of the Sacred Heart only to those souls that are most perfectly abandoned to His will and are destined to the closest union with Him. For it is when these souls by their abandonment have become like wax in God's hands that this likeness of Christ's agony in the garden of Gethsemani is stamped upon them like a seal, or signet.

"God help me!" writes the Carmelite saint, "If for long days and years I considered how great a wrong it is that God should be offended, and that lost souls are His children and my brethren; if I pondered over the dangers of this world and how blessed it would be to leave this wretched life, would not that suffice? [I.e., to make me feel this terrible anguish.] No, daughters, the pain would not be the same. For this [ordinary compunction] by the help of God we can obtain by such meditation. But it does not seem to penetrate the very depths of our being like the other which appears to cut the soul in pieces and grind it to powder through no action — even sometimes with no wish — of its own. What is this sorrow, then? Whence does it come? . . . The soul has so entirely yielded itself into His hands and is so subdued by love for Him that it knows or cares for nothing but that God should dispose of it according to His will. I believe that He only bestows this grace on those He takes entirely for His own."[7]

So terrible a grief took possession of St. Lutgarde that she seems to have suffered on earth many of the pains which are visited upon the souls in purgatory. Indeed, it is likely that she suffered the same kind of pain, and from the same cause. The infused love of God in her soul showed her sin in its true light, and the sight was almost beyond bearing. This was what it meant to be united with Christ! No doubt many pious souls feel a secret ambition for such a union, considering unconsciously rather the honor that it would imply for themselves than their own utter inability to conceive such sufferings, let alone to bear them. Lutgarde was beyond thinking of herself at all. Ground between the upper and nether millstones of pity for sinners and anguish at the outrage of their sins against the perfections of God, she was plunged into an abyss of sorrow that struck all hearts with compassion and awe. Nevertheless, even her tears and anguish betrayed a certain weakness, though certainly no moral imperfection: the very excess of her grief, in the emotional order, sprang from the inability of her soul to bear this close contact with the fire of divine love. But God strengthened her, and raised her to a higher level of peace and self-possession in union with Him.

Christ, therefore, appeared to her in the midst of one of these terrible paroxysms of woe, and gently wiped away her

[7] *The Interior Castle*, V, 2, p. 102.

tears with one of those hands that had been pierced for sinners. He commended her for her love and fidelity, and announced the end of her trial in these words: "I want you now to be consoled and to end these laments for My sinners: nor will I suffer you any longer to exhaust all your strength in weeping. Henceforth you shall continue in prayer with peaceful fervor in your heart. This fervor will suffice to turn aside My Father's wrath as your tears have done hitherto."[8]

It cannot be stressed too much that we are now discussing mystical graces, and that this gift of tears of which St. Lutgarde had just been relieved was strictly a mystical favor of a high order. It must not, therefore, be confused with the gush of tears that spring to the eyes of a fervent postulant who, after a few weeks in the monastery, suddenly discovers that the crucified Christ is really present in the tabernacle, and is there because He loves him with an infinite love. Not that such consolations are to be despised, either: they have their purpose in the wise economy of Providence. They may even be somewhere on the borders of mystical experience, though it would be hard to decide. But St. Aelred of Rievaulx, the great English Cistercian ascetical doctor of the twelfth century, points out that habitual sinners have been known to dissolve into tears before a crucifix at regular intervals, without ever amending their lives.[9]

Both the anguish and the peace that followed were something beyond the control of St. Lutgarde's own will. They were visitations of the Spirit of God, visitations which she could lovingly accept, but could do nothing, directly, to retain or dispel. But Thomas of Cantimpré assures us that once she

---

[8] Consolatam te esse in his lamentis pro meis peccatoribus volo; nec sustinebo te in fletibus ulterius fatigari: sed *placido cordis fervore in oratione persistes;* et per hoc, sicut quondam per lacrymas, iram patris dignanter avertes (*Vita,* 203 d).

[9] Cf. *Speculum Charitatis,* II, 7. He also speaks of those who, in the world of his day, wept copiously over the romance of King Arthur.

entered into this deep and holy tranquillity of soul, that came from a more or less habitual and permanent mystical union with the Sacred Heart, she never lost it again as long as she lived.[10]

The tears and prayers of St. Lutgarde for sinners did more than console the agonizing Christ. The merits of the holy Cistercian were powerful in accomplishing both these works, for there were many converted by her influence from the world to the cloister, and some from tepidity to fervor in the cloister itself.

When we were speaking of her visions of the souls in purgatory, we might have mentioned a certain nun of Aywières whose name was Yolanda. This sister had begun her religious life as a Black Benedictine at the famous convent of Moûtier-sur-Sambre. A woman of noble family and frail health, she had allowed herself to take advantage of the relaxations in that convent, to lead a worldly life, unworthy of her vocation. However, in due time, she began to feel uneasy about this state of affairs, and, stricken with compunction, she consulted St. Lutgarde, who advised her to fly from danger and hide herself behind the walls of Aywières and in the white cowl of a Cistercian nun.

We can guess that Yolanda had many misgivings about her ability to face the rigors of the Cistercian life, but Lutgarde promised to pray earnestly and continuously for her. And she did. She prayed not only that the convert might receive

[10] *Vita,* 203 d. Hic status in ea usque in diem mortis immobilis perduravit. Note that although these accidents of perfect union with God are utterly beyond the reach of the soul, nevertheless St. Teresa teaches that one may, *without graces of infused, or mystical prayer,* attain to a degree equivalent to what she calls "full union" (the "fifth mansion") *by active co-operation with the ordinary grace which is within the reach of all.* And such a one will also possess an inviolable, unshakable peace, although without the special sweetness and delights afforded to mystics. These consolations may make the way to God easier, but they by no means increase our merit, of themselves. Cf. *Interior Castle,* V, 3.

the grace of fervor and strength to lead her new life, but also complete forgiveness of her sins and remission of the temporal punishment due to them. Christ did not refuse to hear these prayers. Yolanda lived a saintly life at Aywières, and at her death the inscription on her tomb called her "beata," "blessed."[11] And, what is more, she was buried in the church, a rare attestation of her holiness of life. She is still commemorated in the Cistercian Menology.[12]

However, the most curious thing about her story is that she, like Jean de Lierre, also entered into an agreement with St. Lutgarde, promising to appear and tell the saint how it was with her after she died. In Yolanda's case, however, it was not so much an agreement, as obedience to a command of the saint, or rather the fulfillment of a prophecy.

Yolanda seems to have looked forward to death with a little misgiving. She had received a supernatural warning that her time was near at hand, and hastened to St. Lutgarde, begging for her prayers. To reassure her that all would be well, the saint told her to remain at peace for, as she said: "I am certain that He will deal with you according to His great mercy, and will quickly deliver you from the punishments of which you are afraid." Then, in confirmation of this statement, Lutgarde prophesied that Yolanda would return after her death and tell her that everything had come out according to her word. "And when you come back," the saint added, "first say 'Benedicite' and then say the Our Father and the Hail Mary, just to make sure that the devil is not mixed up in the affair."

Thomas concludes that everything went according to plan. Yolanda died and barely a month later, while Lutgarde was

---

[11] Cf. a note by the Bollandists, Vita, 199 d, note i.

[12] December 10. The new Menology does not give her credit for an "immemorial cult," although burial in the church might be partial evidence of such a cult. A story that she was a Negress is probably of modern origin, and may simply have resulted from a misunderstanding of the term "monialis nigra," "black nun," meaning Black Benedictine.

at prayer, her former companion appeared to her with a *Benedicite* and said the two prayers. St. Lutgarde hastened to reply with the regular *Dominus* making the conversation official and, so to speak, canonical. Then she at once asked Yolanda how things were going with her in the other world.

"Our Lord did not abhor me in the enormity of my sins," replied the sister. "By thy great grace I obtained mercy." With this she vanished, and left Lutgarde in tears of joy at the infinite mercy of God toward sinners.[13]

Besides the simplicity of St. Lutgarde, an interesting point about this story is the importance attached by her to what may seem, to us, a more or less artificial convention. But the *Benedicite* by which a Cistercian asks permission to break silence is more than a ceremonious way of opening a conversation. St. Lutgarde's attitude shows us that she regarded it as a sacramental: and, as a matter of fact, it is. The two words, *benedicite* and *dominus* are simply the abbreviation of a perished formula by which the one about to speak asked the blessing of the one to whom he was about to speak — usually the prior or Father Abbot. But a blessing is a sacramental. And we can see that St. Lutgarde gave it the importance which is its due, attributing to it, with good reason, the power to keep the devil at a safe distance, if used with the proper intention.

Another nun of Aywières was worried about the soul of her father, a rich nobleman, and one of those of whom Jesus said it was easier for a camel to pass through the eye of a needle than for them to enter into the kingdom of heaven.[14]

She got her father to visit St. Lutgarde, and he begged her to pray that God would give him grace to free himself from the chains of his attachment to money and the things of this world; so Lutgarde consented to adopt him as a kind of

---

[13] *Vita*, 198 e.
[14] Matt. 19:24; Mark 10:25; Luke 18:25.

"spiritual orphan,"[15] and to cherish him with her prayers and intercession before God.

She began to pray for the man's soul. His name was Tymer. Presently one of the other nuns in the convent saw the devil, who was very angry. He said, "So, there goes Mother Lutgarde to deliver Sir Tymer from my chains, in which he has served me these many years! Well, just let her try! She has taken a nice job on her hands. She'll find that she won't be finished in one day. If the worst comes to the worst, I know an easy way to fix *him*. I'll roast his heart in the furnace of poverty, and I'll dry up his soul like a piece of fat in a frying pan."[16] The devils in those days used very graphic language. Nowadays they are content to go about their work without so much noise or complaint—they find so little opposition.

On this occasion, the devil was soon driven to get out the frying pan he had spoken of. Tymer lost all his money and property and was reduced to such a state of poverty that he was hard put to it to avoid complete starvation. In all this, he was as remarkable for his patience and humility as he had been before for his avarice and pride. Finally he received the grace of a religious vocation, and entered the Benedictine monastery of Afflighem[17] where he lived as a saint and died a holy death.

Since we have mentioned Afflighem, we may pass on to a story concerning an abbot of that fervent Benedictine community. It would be a grave error to suppose that all Cluniac

[15] Et se ab illa, sicut in talibus mos est, in spiritualem filium recipi postularet (*Vita*, 201 a).

[16] *Vita*, 201 b.

[17] Afflighem was one of the most famous Cluniac abbeys in the Low Countries. It was founded toward the end of the eleventh century, about the same time as Molesme, and was situated between Brussels and Ghent. It was at Afflighem that St. Bernard was supposed to have saluted a statue of our Lady with "Ave Maria" and received a reply "Salve Bernarde" — a story that is no more than a pious legend, and is nowhere mentioned in the early reliable biographies of the saint. The statue still exists, although the ancient abbey has disappeared. Cf. Migne, P. L., 185, 1800 b.

houses were in a state of decadence. This abbot was a
saintly monk, as well as a close friend and admirer of St.
Lutgarde. One day he brought a man of the world to Aywières
to see the saint, hoping that a word or two from her might do
something for his soul, as he was not leading a Christian
life.

As soon as this person came into the presence of St.
Lutgarde, his face was covered with confusion. The abbot
who was waiting for him outside, was astonished to see him
emerge from the parlor pale and dejected.

"Did you see her?" he asked, wondering what was wrong.

"Yes," came the answer. "I saw her. And I saw something
else, too. I saw in her face something that was like the majesty
of God, and I was filled with such a horror of sin that I have
begged her help that I may get out of the state I am in, and,
with God's grace, never to fall back into it again."

St. Lutgarde was true to her part of the bargain, and he
lived up to his. And his friend the Benedictine abbot bore
witness of this conversion to Thomas of Cantimpré.[18]

If St. Lutgarde exercised a powerful influence, both direct
and indirect, over sinners in the world, she also did even more
by her prayers and advice and example to encourage those who
were weak and suffering temptation in the religious life, particularly in her own austere Order.

One of the crosses of Cistercian life is the absence of human
consolation. There are no purely natural relaxations, no
recreations, no amusements, no diversions. The constant round
of prayer and labor and fasting wearies the flesh, and it was
certainly never designed to afford pleasure to our sensible
appetites. The monk must walk in the dark and love to be
without sensible consolation of any sort. He must love the
sacrifice of all pleasures, even of the seemingly pure delights
of sweetness in prayer. The Cistercian life strips the soul of

18 *Vita*, 201 d.

everything that appeals to the natural faculties of man, whether high or low, and leaves him to walk in pure faith. Under such circumstances, the monk either gets to love his own nothingness, and to love this destitution that simply compels him to depend entirely and blindly on God, or else he gives up the struggle and ends up in the misery of compromise and tepidity. Yet God, in His wise Providence, knows that we need relief and consolation from time to time, and we can be sure that He will give us the graces we need, just as we need them, and when we need them most. If we only knew it, these graces perhaps come to us most often through the prayers of our companions, our fathers in the monastery, our sisters in the convent. Indeed, it is not unlikely that when we get to heaven we shall discover that many of our greatest graces on earth were obtained for us by brothers we were tempted to consider as religious of little account!

There was a nun called Hespelende — another one of those complex Flemish names — who was crushed under an exceedingly heavy and galling burden of temptations. She was nearly in despair. She went to St. Lutgarde and asked for her prayers. The saint, as usual, complied promptly and with the greatest fervor, besieging the throne of God with burning desire and tears. Her simplicity must have been very great indeed to judge by the spontaneous sympathy and love with which she was able to embrace the needs and intentions of sisters and even of utter strangers as if they were her very own. This probably explains the prompt and miraculous answers that were so often granted her.

Hespelende was informed by a prophetic revelation that on Good Friday, at the adoration of the holy Cross, and at the precise moment when the priest would uncover the cross singing: *"Ecce lignum Crucis"* her temptation would leave her and she would be strengthened by God's grace. And that was what happened. Her despair left her, and from

then on she was filled with an unshakable trust in God—
that trust without which there is no true love of God: the
fiducia which is the normal fruition of the Cistercian life of
prayer and self-immolation.[19]

There was another young nun, not of Aywières—her convent is not told us—who labored for long years under some
nameless temptation. She once had a vision in which she was
shown a Cistercian nun to whom, as she was told, she would
owe her liberation from this trial. It was not until many years
later that, happening to visit Aywières, she met and recognized
St. Lutgarde as the one she had seen in her vision: and by
Lutgarde's prayers she was freed. Encouraged by this favor,
she hastened to ask another. She had always had very weak
health, and had always found it extremely difficult to observe the ordinary fasts and abstinence prescribed for people
in the world. It is a wonder that she was admitted to
the Cistercian Order at all, as she was apparently completely
incapable of keeping most of the Rule. However, since
she was still very young, she was allowed every kind of
relief, and was afforded the use of meat. Evidently her
superiors had not been wrong in judging that she had
at least the spirit of her vocation, for there was nothing
she wanted less than to live in the Order without keeping the
Rule, merely subsisting on indulgences: and this was the
subject of her second request to the saint. Vanquished by the
young nun's pitifully sincere entreaties, St. Lutgarde promised
her that from that day forth she would be able to do without

19 Confidence (*fiducia*) plays a role of cardinal importance in the
ascetical and mystical teaching of St. Bernard. It is the *sine qua non* of
mystical union, the marriage of wills with God, which is only effected
by perfect love, and "perfect love casteth out fear . . . he that feareth
is not perfect in charity" (1 John 4:18). This is brought out with especial
clarity in the later teaching of the great Cistercian doctor, for instance
in the 83rd Sermon on the Canticle of Canticles. See also Gilson,
Mystical Theology of St. Bernard, 143, etc. The story of Hespelende
comes in *Vita*, 201 e.

meat, and keep the whole Rule besides. What is more, she added that she would be given the strength to add whatever she desired, in the way of unprescribed mortifications.

Although the fulfillment of this prophecy was perhaps not the *"mirum et stupendum miraculum"*[20] that Thomas of Cantimpré calls it, it was nevertheless quite remarkable. When the young nun returned to her own convent, and went into the refectory of the infirmary to take her dinner, meat was placed before her as usual, but, far from eating it, she could not even bear the sight of it without nausea. Repeated attempts to get her to eat meat only confirmed her in her intense disgust for it, and she never touched it again for the rest of her life. At the same time, all the rest of the Rule became easy, and she was able to add extra mortifications, under obedience, without difficulty.

When this young nun became much older, she was elected abbess of her community, and became acquainted with Thomas of Cantimpré, to whom she avowed all these things with no little shame, which probably accounts for the fact that he did not tell us anything that might have enabled his contemporaries to guess who she was.[21]

On more than one occasion St. Lutgarde proved that she possessed the special gift of supernatural insight into the secrets of souls. For instance, there was a young girl, a recluse of La Cour Saint-Etienne, who came to ask her prayers for help to overcome a temptation. St. Lutgarde asked her what the temptation was. The young girl, laboring under a false shame, was unable to reveal what it was, but it was not necessary for her to do so. The saint told her. And she also told her that the way to overcome her temptation and difficulties was to be frank and open about them in the confessional — for she had also refused to reveal her trouble to the priest.

[20] "A wonderful and astounding miracle" (*Vita*, 201 c).
[21] *Ibidem.*

Not content with helping sinners and harassed nuns and recluses, St. Lutgarde was able to obtain graces for many priests and prelates, and even to give them priceless spiritual advice.

Jacques de Vitry had once been a secular priest at Argenteuil, near Paris. He passed from there into Belgium where he became a religious at the priory of Oignies, and there he undertook the spiritual direction of Bl. Mary of Oignies. Later he entered the newly founded Order of Preachers, followed the Crusaders to Palestine, became first bishop of Acre, then Patriarch of Jerusalem. He was to end his career as Cardinal-Bishop of Tusculum, or Frascati, near Rome. A brilliant, learned, eloquent, and holy man, he played no small part in the mystical ferment of his time, in Belgium, by his preaching, writings, and direction of souls. He was, in fact, one of those theologians who, though probably not himself a mystic, was of the kind St. Teresa recommended so highly as a director of favored souls.[22]

The devil made a subtle attempt to spoil this great career before it was fairly started. It was a temptation to evil under the guise of good, as from an angel of light. He made the priest believe that his interest in one of his penitents was purely spiritual, and urged him on to neglect his preaching in order to devote unnecessary time to earnest conversations with her about the affairs of her soul. Despite his good intentions and the sinlessness of his affection for her, this was nevertheless not supernatural but rather a natural friendship, and therefore dangerous for him in so far as it interfered with his obligations, and constituted a permanent menace to his peace of soul. St. Lutgarde became aware of all this before it ever

[22] It is well known that St. Teresa suffered much from inept confessors who had absolutely no knowledge of ascetic theology and were not capable of guiding souls, and she learned by experience the value of guidance by a good theologian. Cf. her *Life*, especially chapters xxv to xxx; *Interior Castle*, VI. Mansion, VIII, 10–11.

dawned on Jacques himself, and she began to pray for him with her usual intense zeal. Her prayers had no effect. She redoubled her efforts, and began to complain to God, accusing Him of "cruelty" in refusing to answer her. She received a reply from an interior voice saying: "The man for whom you are praying is the one who is defeating your prayers." At this, St. Lutgarde became all the more insistent. Finally, she cried out with a kind of holy impatience: "What art Thou doing, O most kind and most just Lord? Either let me be separated from Thee altogether, or else deliver this man from his attachment, even against his own will." If Lutgarde had been the theologian Jacques de Vitry was, she might have refrained from making such a prayer: and yet it was the prayer of Moses and St. Paul[23] and her holy stubbornness obtained its answer without delay. Jacques de Vitry gave up this dangerous relationship and then, after it was all over, scales fell from his eyes, and he finally realized the peril in which he had placed himself, with all his seemingly pure intentions.

As St. Lutgarde went on in life, growing older in years and progressing further and further in union with God, she developed a more and more vivid and poignant sense of the magnitude and responsibility of the vocation of Christ's priests, and of the failure of some to live up to that vocation. This sense seems to be one of the inevitable consequences of a life of close intimacy with the Sacred Heart: it is a grace which goes hand in hand with that other one, sharing the agony of His love for sinners. Christ has made His Apostles the salt of the earth, and St. Luke tells us what our Lord said about this "salt": "Salt is good, but if the salt shall

---

[23] And returning to the Lord, he [Moses] said: I beseech Thee, this people hath sinned a heinous sin, and they have made to themselves gods of gold: either forgive them this trespass, or if Thou wilt not, strike me out of the book which Thou hast written (Exod. 32:31–32). For I wished myself to be an anathema from Christ, for my brethren, who are my kinsmen according to the flesh (Rom. 9:3).

lose its savor, wherewith shall it be seasoned? It is neither profitable for the land nor for the dunghill, but shall be cast out. He that hath ears to hear, let him hear."[24]

It is interesting to contrast this more forceful statement of the same thing with the version given by Matthew in a different context.[25] In Matthew, the "loss of savor" by the salt is the failure to do good works. In Luke, the context is more specific — and even more arresting. The sentence comes as the climax and conclusion of a series of forceful commands of Jesus to His chosen disciples. They must hate their father and mother and their wife and children and their own life also, or they cannot be His disciples. "And," Jesus added, "whosoever doth not carry his cross, and come after Me, cannot be My disciple. . . . Every one of you that doth not renounce all that he possesseth, cannot be My disciple."[26] It may be possible for some to doubt just how much detachment is demanded of ordinary Christians as a matter of precept: but such unmistakable words as these allow of no escape from the obligation of priests and religious to an uncompromising renunciation of the world.

St. Lutgarde, in her cloister, had learned of the tragedy of tepidity and negligence and apostasy among priests in more than one way: partly by contact with souls, and partly from the Sacred Heart of Jesus, speaking to her in the silence and secrecy of her inmost soul, complaining of the ingratitude and infidelity of some of His elect.

No one who is at all familiar with the spirituality of great contemplative and cloistered saints of modern times, from St. Margaret Mary to St. Thérèse of Lisieux, will be surprised at the prominence of this urge to pray and make sacrifices for priests, in the spirituality of a Cistercian mystic.

Nevertheless, with St. Lutgarde it was something new.

[24] Luke 14:34–35.   [25] Matt. 5:13.   [26] Luke 24:27, 33.

Not that she was an innovator in this respect: but few there were, before the thirteenth century, who had been inspired with a clear and definite awareness of the Sacred Heart's desire for victim souls to pray and make sacrifices for the sanctification of His priests. This was to become a definitely modern feature in Christian spirituality. With Lutgarde, it is still in its beginnings. But the breakdown of medieval Christianity would create a great demand for souls like hers!

St. Lutgarde was filled with an extreme solicitude for priests, and she used all her influence upon those whom she knew, and who came to visit and consult her at Aywières. She kept telling them to strive after perfection and to give everything they had to their divinely appointed work for the salvation of souls. And she herself received the grace to speak, on such occasions, in words full of fire and unction.[27]

We have seen in what veneration she was held by a priest like Jean de Lierre. We have beheld the effect of her influence in the life of the zealous and holy Jacques de Vitry. Through such men as these, priests of great natural talent and endowed with even greater graces, St. Lutgarde, perhaps far more than she realized, worked powerfully in the Church in Belgium, and even throughout Europe. We have only to mention that when the great Cistercian Bishop of Toulouse, Foulques de Marseille, the converted troubadour and former abbot of Toronet in the sunny coastal mountains of Provence, came to Belgium, he was brought by Jacques de Vitry to visit St. Lutgarde and came away profoundly impressed.[28]

---

[27] Solicita supra modum pia Lutgardis fuit notos sacerdotes cum mira oris gratia frequentius admonere, gregem sibi creditam solicite procurare, et animas, quas Christus redemit, a servitute daemonum liberare (*Vita*, 202 f).

[28] The impression made on Foulques by the holy women he saw in the convents and hermitages of the Low Countries made him insist that Jacques de Vitry set down on paper the life of Bl. Mary of Oignies. Cf. the Cardinal's letter to Foulques, in the preface to Nimal's *"Grandes Saintes du Pays de Liège,"* p. iii.

When St. Lutgarde met Bishop Foulques of Toulouse, she was speaking to a man who was in a key position in the French Church, not because of nobility or dignity (although he possessed both) but because of the burden he bore and the issues that depended on him. Bishop of the most turbulent and difficult see in Christendom, he was fighting heroically against the Albigensian heresy. Ultimately, it was to Foulques more than to any man on earth outside St. Dominic himself that we owe the existence of the Order of Preachers, which first saw the light in the diocese and city of Toulouse under the patronage of the Cistercian bishop.[29]

But perhaps there was no priest who owed more to St. Lutgarde than her own biographer. Thomas of Cantimpré was himself her spiritual son. He consulted her in every difficulty, and followed her guidance for many years, although it was he, officially, who was *her* director.

He tells us[30] that when he was still a young priest, in the days before he entered the Order of Preachers — he began the religious life as a regular Canon — he was delegated to hear reserved cases in the confessional. In other words, his learning as a canonist and moral theologian had earned him a position in which he had to weigh and assess the most difficult and most unpleasant matters of conscience. This task proved to be an immense burden to him, and he frequently came out of the confessional with his feelings in revolt or in turmoil. The evils to which he had had to listen pursued him and haunted his imagination, until he began to be filled with fear and misgiving about the safety of his own conscience. His only remedy was to hasten to his "spiritual mother."[31] St. Lutgarde set his mind at peace with a confident promise that

29 Cf. P. Mandonnet, O.P., St. *Dominic and his Work*, St. Louis, 1944, pp. 368, 373 f.

30 *Vita*, 202 f.

31 Maximo ergo timore et horrore correptus, ad piam Lutgardem, sicut ad specialissimam mihi matrem, accessi . . . (*Vita*, 203 a).

he would receive special graces in the future. "Go back to your work, my son," she told him, "and do all that you must do for the care of souls: Christ will be by your side to protect you and to tell you what to say. When you are hearing confessions, He will not only ward off the missiles of the enemy with His great power, but He will make up for the lack of science, which you fear, with a greater abundance of grace."[32]

Whether, as in the case of the man whom she saved from despair by the mere light of her countenance, Lutgarde acted by her presence alone, or whether she gave the benefit of her heavenly wisdom and her prayers, as she did for example to the poor to whom she had nothing else to give personally, or to the young Benedictine priest of Afflighem who was sent to take charge of a dissolute and intractable parish, St. Lutgarde shed everywhere around her the light of grace and the consolations of the Holy Spirit.[33]

And although she had no learning, that fact alone only served to make the advice she gave, on certain occasions, all the more remarkable to those who received it. She did not understand Latin, she could scarcely make out a word of the Scriptures, and yet, guided by a kind of instinct, she would sometimes come out with a line or a phrase from Holy Writ that so astonished everyone by its fitness that many took her utterances as prophetic and inspired.

Very frequently the voice of the Holy Spirit would suggest these phrases to her, just when they were needed to clarify a situation. Often enough she would utter the words and they would have their effect, and then, when she was alone, she would hasten in her simplicity to find out what they meant.

There are few more charming stories in the life of the saint than that of her alms to a beggar woman. Lutgarde

[32] *Ibidem.*
[33] Cf. *Vita,* 201 f; 202 a, b.

saw a poor old woman, and was moved with pity and an earnest desire to give her something: but, of course, she had nothing to give. Then Christ spoke to her in her heart, saying: "In the psalms that you sing, you say to Me: *'Portio mea, Domine,* O Lord, my portion, I have said, I will keep Thy law.' And that means that I am your portion, I am all that you have, and you have nothing else. So go and tell the poor woman that silver and gold you have none, but what you have, you will give her: for you have kept My law!"

If, along with her gift, St. Lutgarde was able to impart to the poor woman one hundredth part of her own understanding of how much it meant, she must have made her very happy that day! For the soul of the saint herself was flooded with a splendid light, the realization that she not only possessed Christ by love, but could give Him, the beginning and end of everything, to other people! She could give to souls not a mere earthly alms, not an earthly treasure, but the treasure of the infinite glory and wisdom and love of the eternal God!

She hastened home, and told her learned sister, Sybil de Gages, of what had been spoken to her in her heart, and together they started paging through a commentary on the Psalms, to see how this interpretation fitted in with the Fathers of the Church. Sybil was skeptical at first, but to her surprise and delight she discovered that Lutgarde's interior voice was, indeed, perfectly orthodox.

CHAPTER SIX

THE SPIRITUALITY OF ST. LUTGARDE. HER MYSTICISM

EVER since the days of the early Christians, when St. Paul had to warn the Colossians against the dangers of false mysticism, the Church has had to contend with the dangerous attraction which some of her most fervent children seem to find in systems of spirituality that are so "pure" that they even exclude the humanity of Jesus from the meditations of their adepts. Among sixty-eight propositions of the quietist Miguel Molinos, condemned in 1687 by Innocent XI, we read the following: "Souls that follow the interior way must not elicit acts of love for the Blessed Virgin, or for the saints, or for the humanity of Christ, because, since all these objects are sensible, love for them is also sensible."[1]

This error sprang from a false conception of purity of heart, which demanded the utter exclusion of all sensible images, all phantasms, all ideas, all notions, distinct or otherwise, of God in His Incarnation or in Himself, from the mind of anyone seeking union with Him. Purity of heart meant simply the annihilation of the faculties. The only way to reach God was, according to these men, utterly to destroy one's intellect and will by a total cessation of all operation on their part, so that the soul became inert in the hands of God.

---

[1] Prop. 36. See Denzinger-Bannwart, *Enchiridion Symbolorum*, No. 1255.

The great theologians teach that the only possible way a rational creature can be united to God is by the operation of some faculty. We are united to God by faith, hope, and love and these require acts of our intellect and will.

But the only way in which we can rise to a supernatural love of God is through loving faith in Jesus, the Son of God, in whom we behold the visible and tangible evidence of God's love for us, especially in His Passion and death, and from whom we receive the grace to correspond to His infinite love.

"I am the way, the truth and the life," said Jesus.[2] "No man cometh to the Father but by Me. . . ." "He that seeth Me, seeth the Father also."[3]

And the Disciple St. John gives us, in clear and unmistakable terms, a standard by which to test false systems of spirituality: "Dearly beloved," he writes,[4] "believe not every spirit, but try the spirits, if they be of God; because many false prophets are gone out into the world. By this is the spirit of God known. Every spirit which confesseth that Jesus Christ is come in the flesh, is of God. And every spirit that dissolveth Jesus, is not of God. And this is Antichrist, of whom you have heard that he cometh, and he is now already in the world." "He that hath the Son, hath life, and he that hath not the Son, hath not life."[5]

It is clear, then, how insidious and terrible is the danger of a doctrine that would have us put Christ and His Passion out of our minds, forget Him and His saints and His Blessed Mother, cease to reflect upon the greatness and goodness of God, or upon the Blessed Trinity dwelling within us, and, if we receive the sacraments at all, receive them in a state of spiritual coma, without recognition, without love, without response. Not, of course, that everyone has to force his mind every instant to produce rational considerations or elaborate affections upon all these subjects, for to do so might also

[2] John 14:6.   [3] John 14:9.   [4] 1 John 4:1-3.   [5] 1 John 5:12.

mean a partial sterilization of grace in the soul, under certain circumstances. It is clear that those who have progressed a certain distance in the interior life not only seldom need to make systematic meditations, but rather profit by abandoning them in favor of a simple and peaceful affective prayer, without fuss, without noise, without much speech, and with no more than one or two favorite ideas or mysteries, to which they return in a more or less general and indistinct manner each time they pray.

The main thing is to establish contact with God by loving faith. This implies at least enough awareness for the mind to be alive to the presence of God, and to the nearness of Jesus to our souls, and whatever keeps that awareness fresh in our hearts must be sought and encouraged. Hence, we must love the Holy Scriptures, and read them assiduously. We must keep immersed in the liturgy, and remain close to the tabernacle. Above all, we must faithfully and constantly strive to improve the quality of our participation in the infinitely holy and powerful Sacrifice of the Mass. All these will have the effect of keeping the humanity of Jesus before our eyes, and close to our hearts, if we only take advantage of them. And these are the foundation stones of Cistercian spirituality and mysticism.

On the other hand, the humanity of Jesus, His sacraments, and the sacramental and liturgical life of His Church as a whole, had been abandoned by the Albigensians of St. Lutgarde's time in favor of what they considered a purer spirituality. We have seen how their manichaean brand of natural mysticism strove, like that of the quietists, their lineal descendants, to "annihilate" human nature, instead of lending it to the peaceful and merciful operations of grace, by which it might quickly reach its full supernatural development and ascend to heights of perfection far beyond the scope of our own powers.

If nothing else is clear from the pages that have so far been written in this book, at least we have seen that the whole interior life of St. Lutgarde centered upon the Sacred Heart of Jesus. The humanity of Christ had been abandoned and scorned by men who thought themselves spiritual, and who aspired to high mysticism without Him. It was Lutgarde's vocation, as a true Christian mystic, to make reparation for that blasphemous folly by an intense and simple and hidden love for the Son of Mary, for Jesus who was born in human flesh, with the mind and soul and Heart of a man, and who died for His brothers on the Cross. Her love for Jesus did not have to be raised up by great flights of intellectual speculation concerning the union of the divine and human Natures in His Person. She loved the Christ she saw on the Cross, and her faith told her that He was God. Thus she arrived simply and directly, by the guidance of His Spirit, through the Gospels, the liturgy, the sacraments, at the possession of the infinite God by love, while the Albigensians, with their fierce Oriental gymnastics of the spirit, never got any nearer to heaven than the limits of their own imagination. Perhaps they managed, on occasion, to hypnotize themselves into a feeble counterfeit of ecstasy by dint of sheer concentration.

The errors of the Cathari have survived in many forms: there are still many and grave temptations that assail the soul that is attracted to seek God in the ways of prayer. We tend to forget the Gospels and to wander away after false prophets, enticed by the illusion of grandiose and subtle methods of embellishing our souls, with mystical experiences, and all the time we forget that these things are not in our own power. We forget the warning of St. Paul: "Let no one cheat you who takes pleasure in self-abasement and worship of angels, and enters vainly into what he has not seen, puffed up by his mere human mind. Such a one is not united to the head, from whom the whole body, supplied and built up by joints and ligaments, attains a growth that is of God."[6]

Let us rather seek the Word of life, that we may rejoice in Him, and that our joy may be full. It is the Apostles who will give us this good Word, uttered from the heart of God: "That which was from the beginning, which we have heard, which we have seen with our eyes, which we have looked upon, and our hands have handled, of the word of life: for the life was manifested, and we have seen, and do bear witness, and declare unto you the life eternal, which was with the Father, and hath appeared to us."[7]

And in Him we will truly live and be glad, and seeing Jesus and believing Him, the seeds of glory will be planted and spring up in our souls.

This was the spirituality, the mysticism of St. Lutgarde. It is the basis of the spirituality of Citeaux. The love of Christ, to whom "nothing is to be preferred"[8] is the foundation of the Benedictine Rule. But love cannot be idle, it must act. Not, of course, that it has to pour itself out in external, physical activity: for the highest form of spiritual love far transcends that imperfect notion of activity which includes external motion and change. This is perhaps why the love of the contemplative for God seems to the active man to be idleness. On the contrary, it is a far more intense, and powerful, and fruitful activity, because it is spiritual and hidden. It is closer to the activity of angels than to that of mortal men: it belongs to heaven rather than to the earth.

Paradoxically, this contemplative love is perfect activity and yet perfect repose — a paradox which Duns Scotus explains in his discussion of beatitude. The Subtle Doctor points

---

[6] Col. 2:18 (New Revised Version).
[7] 1 John 1:1-2.
[8] Rule of St. Benedict, IV, 21.

out that any conception of heaven which conceives activity
and rest as succeeding one another as we enter there, is based
on an imperfect and human metaphor from physical motion.
Actually, the activity by which we love God with all the
power of our being in heaven, is precisely our *rest* in heaven.
We can never rest until our nature receives this perfect
fulfillment in total and unimpeded and free activity, because,
for Scotus, rest cannot consist in inertia but in *fulfillment,
freedom.* And only in heaven is the will at last perfectly free
of all those imperfections and defects which act as brakes
and obstacles impeding the one activity for which it was
created: the love of God for His own sake. "It is the same
operation which at the same time perfectly attains to the object
[God] and rests in Him, because we rest precisely in this
perfect attainment of our object. . . ." "An operative power
does not rest in its object, *except by that perfect operation in
which it attains to the object.*"[9]

In the third book of his *Speculum Charitatis*, the great
English Cistercian theologian, St. Aelred of Rievaulx, expresses much the same idea of union with God by love in
his exposition of the three degrees of the interior life as three
"Sabbaths," or three degrees of rest. The first, corresponding
to the "Purgative Way" is the less perfect in terms of rest
because there is more external activity. The great multiplicity
of objects and appetites that stand between us and God im-
pede the direct flight of our love to Him, and we are busy
struggling to keep from being overwhelmed by temptations.
In the second "Sabbath," we reach the stage where we
"rest" in the more perfect union of a fraternal charity that
brings peace with all our brethren, and delivers us, from
all conflict with them: a peace that would never have

[9] Eadem operatio hic est assecutiva perfecte et quietativa, quia quietatio
est in perfecta assecutione objecti . . . potentia operativa non quietatur in
objecto, nisi per operationem perfectam per quam attingit objectum (IV,
Ox. d. 49, q. 4).

been possible if we had not first established peace within ourselves. But this second degree of peace prepares the way for the third and final step: immediate union with God Himself. Here, at last, our love becomes most perfect in its activity, because it is unified, concentrated on God alone, and not separated and divided among a multiplicity of objects. Hence, we have perfect activity and perfect quietude.

"And because in unity there is no division, in this state the mind is not poured out among many things. Its activity is all centered in One, with One, through One, about One: it sees One alone, enjoys One alone: and because this object is always One, the soul is always resting. And thus does it celebrate its everlasting Sabbath."[10]

When Thomas of Cantimpré comes to discuss the mysticism of St. Lutgarde, he does so in terms which show that he was steeped in the traditions of the Cistercian school. St. Bernard and his disciples, great and small, from St. Aelred to men like Baldwin of Ford and Gilbert of Hoyland, delighted in allegories of the various stages of the interior life. Three is their favorite number, according to the traditional division of the three ways, purgative, illuminative, and unitive. However, Thomas of Cantimpré treats the subject in a way that seems to indicate a special influence of St. Aelred's *Speculum Charitatis*. There would be nothing strange in this. St. Aelred was widely read on the Continent, and one of his works, *De Spirituali Amicitia*, was translated into French by the courtly Jehan de Meung.[11]

St. Aelred brings in his three degrees, with slightly different variations, in the second and third books of the *Speculum*.

---

[10] Et quia in unitate nulla est divisio, nulla sit ibi per diversa mentis effusio: sed sit unum in uno cum uno, per unum, circa unum: unum sentiens, unum sapiens; et quia semper unum, semper requiescens: et sic perenne sabbatum sabbatizans (St. Aelred, *Speculum Charitatis*, III, 1, Migne, P. L., 195, 576 d).

[11] *Collectanea O.C.R. Annus II*, p. 123. "Le Bienheureux Aelred," by Camille Hontoir, O.C.R.

In the third he introduces his Cistercian monks to three "sabbaths," or three degrees of "rest" as we have seen. In the second book, speaking more particularly of the life of prayer, he gives three degrees of prayer. In the first degree he deals with the consolations and lights given to beginners; in the second, to the trials and darkness and aridity, alternating with stronger and purer graces, granted to the progressives, to strengthen and purify them; and in the third he discusses the contemplation and union which complete the ascent.

Thomas of Cantimpré's three *lectuli*, or "beds," seem to be a combination of both of these systems in St. Aelred. He got these beds from the Canticle of Canticles. "In my bed by night I sought Him whom my soul loveth."[12] "Behold threescore valiant ones of the most valiant of Israel, surrounded the bed of Solomon,"[13] and *"lectulus noster floridus*: our bed is flowery, full of flowers."[14]

"The first of these beds," he says, "signifies the state of penance, which is the state of beginners. The second, the state of combat, proper to progressives, and the third, the state of the contemplative life (that is, habitual union with God, the constant sense of His presence, and perfect harmony with His will), and this is the state of the perfect."[15]

Summing up St. Lutgarde's whole life, her Dominican biographer assures us that although she never had to atone for any mortal sin, nevertheless she sought her Beloved in the ways of penance and contrition, weeping for her semideliberate faults and imperfections and for the sins of the world. Hers was not the false mysticism of the quietists who,

[12] Cant. 3:1.
[13] Cant. 3:7.
[14] Cant. 1:15. The Douay translators' "flourishing" no longer conveys the idea of *floridus*.
[15] Primus lectulus comparatur statui poenitentiae; qui est status inchoantium: secundus statui pugnae; qui est status proficientium; tertius status vitae contemplativae, qui est status perfectorum (*Vita*, 203 f). Cf. St. Thomas, "Vita contemplativa est propria perfectorum," II. II. 2. 182, a. 4, ad 1.

refusing to accept anything that might disturb their own self-complacency, deliberately studied and cultivated indifference to sin, and cauterized their conscience against every feeling of shame, on the grounds that all reflection and introspection were merely unregenerate self-love, no matter for what purpose they were practiced.[16]

St. Teresa tells us that it is a great mistake to suppose that those who are closely united to God have ceased to think about their sins, and are never affected by the memory of them. On the contrary, "sorrow for sin increases in proportion to the divine grace received" and the past errors of such souls seem to them madness and folly which they never cease to lament, not so much because of the fear of hell — for that fear, indeed, has all but left them — but because of their great ingratitude to God.[17]

From this we may judge that the first *"lectulum"* in Thomas' series is not to be taken literally as the degree of an ordinary beginner, for it is quite evident that St. Lutgarde's compunction was a mystical grace, a fact of which Thomas himself was conscious, and which makes his three degrees somewhat misleading. So, too, the state of combat was, for St. Lutgarde, something far beyond the ordinary state of a progressive in the ways of virtue. This is manifest from the quasimiraculous character of her seven-year fasts, and Thomas admits it when he says that the sixty valiants who surrounded her symbolized not only the angels, who sometimes visibly came to her assistance, as we shall see, but also the saints and the Blessed Virgin herself.

In the third stage, St. Lutgarde has ascended beyond the angels, and arrived at immediate union with the Word of God. This distinction, far from being merely fanciful, is

[16] Condemned propositions of Miguel Molinos, Denzinger-Bannwart, 1227, 1228, 1229, 1230, 1231, etc.
[17] *Interior Castle*, VI Mansions, chap. vii, 1–5.

something strictly technical in mystical theology, but it is difficult to say how much Thomas of Cantimpré means by it here. St. John of the Cross, in the *Living Flame of Love* (Stanza 2, lines 1 and 2), explains in minute detail the difference between the effect produced in the soul by God through the mediation of an angelic spirit, and by the immediate contact of the divine Substance: but the problem of establishing whether or not it would have been easy for a thirteenth-century theologian to have gathered such truths by ordinary means from the writings of the Fathers and whatever else was at his disposal, would lead us far outside the scope of the present work.

Thomas sums up St. Lutgarde's mystical union with God in the following more or less conventional terms[18] which, translated into the language of St. Teresa, might mean anything from ordinary mystical union to the mystical marriage: "Her spirit was so absorbed in God that she was overwhelmed with amazement, like the Queen of Sheba and lost possession of her faculties; but, being totally translated into God, like a drop of water in a jar of wine, she became one spirit with Him. And this is what Christ, as He was about to enter upon His Passion, prayed His Father to grant to all who should believe in Him, saying: As Thou, Father, in Me, and I in Thee, so they may be one in Us."[19]

The Dominican writer's language in this passage is general enough and conventional enough to give us some idea of St. Lutgarde's union with God. But it is not very precise. As a

[18] Ita spiritus ejus absorbebatur in Deum (does he mean continually and habitually, or from time to time?), ut cum Regina Saba in admiratione deficiens (*admiratio* can mean the overwhelming of the faculties by the divine light in such a way as to produce ecstasy), ultra spiritum non haberet. (In mystical marriage, there are periods of greater absorption in God, but the soul is never completely bereft of contact with the world, as in lower degrees, cf. St. Teresa, VII Mansions.) Sed tota translata in Deum, instar guttae aquae in dolium vini, unus cum eo spiritus miscebatur (*Vita*, 204 a).

[19] John 20:21.

matter of fact, it tells us more about her biographer than it does about herself. It gives us, as we have seen, an insight into his theological background, but what is more arresting is the quotation with which he brings to a close this discussion, and, in fact, the whole second book of the *Life*. He insists that this intimate union with God is something which Christ Himself begged His Father to give to those who should believe in Him. Not only that, but He did so at the Last Supper, the night before His Passion: *"Et hoc est quod Christus ad passionem properans a Patre pro his qui credituri essent petiit."* He adds the words we have quoted to make it a solid theological proof: "As Thou Father in Me, and I in Thee, that they may be one in Us." We know that this was the prayer of Christ, and we know that it means the closest possible kind of union, and we know that He asked it "for them also who through their [the Apostles'] word shall believe in Me." Thomas gives a particular urgency to the prayer with the *properans,* Christ *hastening* to His Passion. It recalls our Lord's own words: "With desire I have desired to eat this pasch with you before I suffer."[20]

St. Bernard taught his monks that this union could be had even in this life, by those who forsook all things, and gave themselves up entirely to love of Christ.[21]

Here is how St. Lutgarde saw Christ in her visions.

"In an instant," she told Thomas, "His inestimable splendor appears to me, and I see, as it were in a flash of lightning, the inexpressible beauty of His glory. And if the vision of Him did not rapidly pass from my sight, I would no longer be able to sustain it, but I should surely die."[22]

---

[20] Luke 22:15.

[21] St. Bernard, *Sermo.* xxxii and lxxxiii, in *Cantica.*

[22] In momento apparet mihi splendor inaestimabilis et quasi fulgur video ejus ineffabilem pulchritudinem glorificationis; quae nisi raptim transiret ab aspectu contemplationis meae, cum vita praesenti hanc sustinere non possem (*Vita,* 206 d). *Glorificatio* means Christ's glorified body. However,

The saint then went on to explain how, though the vision itself passed quickly, it left behind a species deeply impressed in the memory — a species which, in itself, must have surpassed in vividness and spiritual power any of the graces of a lower mystical order. Nevertheless, compared with the direct vision of Christ Himself, this indirect contact with Him through the memory was as nothing, and served rather to fill her soul with the anguish of separation from Him whom she had just seen in all His glory, but who had vanished as quickly as He had come.

"After the blazing light of that vision," St. Lutgarde said, "there remains an intellectual splendor: and when, in that splendor, I look for Him whom I saw for that brief instant, I find Him not."

What was most impressive about this vision was not its sensible, physical beauty, but the spiritual, intelligible splendor which nevertheless eminently contained all the perfections of a lower order of beauty.

St. John of the Cross describes an intellectual vision in much the same terms: "It is as though one saw a door of light thrown open, giving the impression of a flash of lightning which suddenly discloses the whole extent of all that is to be seen, dispelling the darkness of the night. For an instant, all the details are seen with a most marvelous precision, and then the night falls again, but the forms and outlines remain in the imagination."[23]

Commenting on all this — Thomas of Cantimpré finds that it illustrates a line from the fifth chapter of the Canticle of Canticles: "My soul melted when he spoke: I sought him, and found him not: I called and he did not answer me."[24]

---

there is question here only of an intellectual vision, not of a corporeal vision of that body.

[23] St. John of the Cross, *Ascent of Mount Carmel*, ii, 22.
[24] Cant. 5:6.

Christ, says the Dominican confessor of our saint, shows Himself to the soul in order to give her an idea of His immense perfections, and so to impress upon her how great a height of sanctity she must aspire to in order to be united to Him. Then He vanishes, in order that she may desire Him all the more ardently, and seek Him with ever increasing fervor.[25] This is substantially the teaching of St. Bernard and of practically all mystical doctors concerning the comings and goings of the Word, visiting and touching the soul with special graces and then departing once more, leaving it burning with a deeper and more scalding wound of love than before.[26]

St. Teresa, writing three hundred years after St. Lutgarde, describes the same experience in the same words, except that what St. John of the Cross and Thomas of Cantimpré class as "spiritual" and "intellectual" she calls "imaginative."

"Christ shows the soul in vision His most sacred humanity," writes the great Carmelite, "under whatever form He chooses: either as He was during His life here on earth, or after His resurrection. The vision passes as quickly as a flash of lightning, yet this most glorious picture makes an impression on the imagination that I believe can never be effaced until the soul at last sees Christ to enjoy Him forever. Although I call it a 'picture,' you must not imagine that it looks like a painting; Christ appears as a living person, Who sometimes speaks and reveals deep mysteries. You must understand that though the soul sees this for a certain space of time, it is no

[25] Quid est Christum loqui in anima nisi repraesentare illi suae divitias bonitatis, sapientiae et decoris? Ut ex his metiatur anima, quam bonum, quamque sapientem, et a virtutibus decoratum eum esse oporteat, qui ejus amorem poterit in caritate perpetua promereri. Hunc ergo audiens, anima liquescit in desideriis, et nititur obtinere quem conspicit; sed quia tempus perfectae visionis nondum venit, illum quem quasi praesentem habuit, subito perdit; ut tanto diligentius quaerat, quanto ardentius amat; et tanto ad possidendum mens latior praeparetur, quanto ad quaerendum frequentius innovatur (*Vita*, 206 d).

[26] See St. Bernard, *Sermons on the Cant. of Canticles*, especially Nos. 31, 74. St. Teresa, *Interior Castle*, VI Mans., chap. 11.

more possible to continue looking at it than to gaze for a very long time on the sun; therefore this vision passes very quickly, although its brightness does not pain the interior sight in the same way as the sun's glare injures our bodily eyes."[27]

We cannot refrain, at this point, from quoting St. Teresa's warning to those who imagine they have such experiences, without actually receiving anything of the kind. A lively imagination, coupled with a rather vague concept of faith, which endows mere fancies with a pseudo-supernatural conviction, can produce interior voices, locutions, and even visions of a sort. If the victim is persistent enough and stubborn enough, he can keep this up long enough to produce a fairly plausible sounding spiritual autobiography every second page of which begins with some fresh communication from heaven. These things may be simply the product of a combination of natural talent and sincere, but misguided conscience. If the soul is really pious and devoted to the duties of her state, she may even do a little good by her fancied messages from heaven, but it will only be the fruit of imagination and ingenuity, rather than of faith and grace. On the other hand, since the devil likes nothing better than to take advantage of these things for his own purposes, visions should never be encouraged or desired. This is the clear and unanimous teaching of all Christian mystical theologians. However, since visions and other *gratiae gratis datae* are mere accidents of the mystical life, there is no reason why a fervent soul should not aspire to *true* mystical union with God.

Writing in the latter part of her life, when she was acquainted with every possible kind of mystical experience, and, what is more important in a foundress, possessed deep supernatural insight into souls, St. Teresa said that not three or four but scores of people had come to her to

[27] *Interior Castle*, **VI** Mans., chap. ix, No. 2, Stanbrook translation, p. 203.

tell her all about the visions they were having. "I know by experience," she said, "that there are souls which, because they possess vivid imaginations or active minds, or for some other reason of which I am ignorant, are so absorbed in their own ideas as to feel certain they *see* whatever their fancy imagines. If they had ever beheld a genuine vision, they would recognize the deception unmistakably. They themselves fabricate, piece by piece, what they fancy they see: no after effects are produced on the mind, which is less moved to devotion than by the sight of a sacred picture. It is clear that no attention should be paid to such fancies, which pass more quickly than dreams from the memory."

One must not suppose, either, that St. Teresa despised holy pictures. She probably got as much out of them as anyone could get.[28] Nevertheless, she pointed out that there was and there could be simply no thought of comparing natural and sensible images and feelings with the tremendous effect on the soul of such a vision as has been described. In the first place, it always resulted in rapture or ecstasy, according to the Saint of Ávila, who likened the experience to that of St. Paul on the road to Damascus.[29] Then, also, the effect on the soul was always an enduring growth in sanctity. Once she had seen the Face of Christ in glory, St. Teresa felt it was almost beyond physical power to commit a sin, for, as she said: "I sincerely assure you that, wicked as I am, I have never feared the torments of hell, for they have seemed to me as nothing when I remembered that the lost would see the beautiful meek and pitiful eyes of the Lord turned on them in wrath. I have thought all my life that this would be more than my heart could bear."[30]

To return to the charismata of St. Lutgarde: she, too, like

[28] See her *Autobiography, passim,* especially Chap. xxii.
[29] *Interior Castle,* VI Mans., ix, 7. Acts 9:3–8.
[30] *Ibid.,* ix, 4.

St. Teresa, had been completely enraptured with the sight
of the eyes of Christ, concerning which the dying Patriarch
Jacob had cried in prophecy: "His eyes are more beautiful
than wine."[31] She described the glory of her vision by saying
that if one could imagine a light that outshone the sun as
the sun outshone the stars, that would still fall infinitely short
of the brightness of the eyes of Christ.[32]

Once St. Lutgarde was deep in contemplation, when one
of the other sisters heard a voice above the head of the saint,
saying: "My delights are to be with the children of men."
This did not surprise her Dominican confessor. He called St.
Augustine to witness that the soul purified by faith and good
works is a paradise where God takes up His abode and loves
to dwell. And then, he adds, the re-creation of the fallen
human soul by the Redemption was something far greater
than the creation of the world out of nothing, if we are to
judge by the labor and sufferings and the bitter agony and
death which the Incarnate Word of God underwent in order
to bring it to completion. But, Thomas concludes, if all this
is true of the ordinary Christian in the state of grace, how
much more is it so of a saint purified, like Lutgarde, by years
of sacrifice, of interior and exterior trials and crosses, sustained
with the most perfect and most ardent love? "If this be so,
what could possibly have been more delightful to Christ, the
Son of God, in our times, than Lutgarde? If anything was,
I know it not, God knows. But one thing I do know: I have
believed, therefore I have spoken, and confess that I cannot
remember ever having heard or read of anyone like her!"
The simplicity and enthusiasm of these words are characteristic of the Dominican who was at the same time Lutgarde's
spiritual father and her spiritual son.[33]

[31] Gen. 49:12.
[32] Vita, 206 e.
[33] Quid Christo Dei Filio nostris temporibus delicatius esse potuit quam
Lutgardis: Si fuerit, nescio; Deus scit. Unum scio, credidi propter quod

We know that many of the saints had enemies. They knew what it was to be hated, mistrusted, and persecuted. Few of them escaped the envy and jealousy of their fellow men.

In several passages of the *Vita Lutgardis,* Thomas of Cantimpré intimates somewhat obscurely that even at Aywières St. Lutgarde had to bear with the coldness, envy, and ill-concealed hostility of some of her sisters in religion. He does not go so far as to say that she had to face violent opposition, still less that she suffered injustice or persecution. Nor did the jealousy of a few sisters at Aywières compare with the public and almost universal criticism she had once received from the nuns at St. Catherine's.

Nevertheless, Lutgarde was criticized. She was certainly a very unusual person. True, we find little or no eccentricity in her character — which is more than can be said for some saints. Her ecstasies do not appear to have constituted a real nuisance in the community. She was not like Bl. Ida of Louvain who, having acquired great fame as a mystic in the world, became a Cistercian nun at Roosendael. Bl. Ida used to receive Communion with the rest of the nuns at the high altar but, being unable to return to her place in choir with the rest, she would find her way around behind the altar and sit down on the floor in ecstasy until Mass and the Office of Sext were over. Bl. Ida of Léau and several other Cistercian nuns of La Ramée, another Belgian convent, also used to be caught up in rapture after receiving Communion. Their less exalted sisters had to carry them back from the altar to their places in choir.[34]

St. Lutgarde does not seem to have created any such scenes. Nevertheless, as she grew older and gave way under the burden of sickness, she did need someone to help her

---

locutus sum, quod nullam me talem vel legisse meminerim vel audisse (*Vita,* 207 a).

[34] Cf. the Life of Bl. Ida of Louvain, *Acta Sanctorum,* April, ii, and that of Bl. Ida of Léau, *ibid.,* October, xiii.

up to the high altar when she went to Communion. Her Dominican biographer does not tell us in so many words that some of her sisters who might have performed this office for her refused to do so out of spite: but he does say that she was seen to ascend the altar, when no one else would help her, supported by two angels, "in order that her merits might be shown to those at Aywières who, perhaps, did not entertain thoughts that were worthy of her."[35]

The situation, however, must be clarified. For these things happened, not on days of general Communion when all the nuns ascended the altar in procession, but when Lutgarde went to Communion all alone. The fact is, that the saint was the only one in the convent who received the Body and Blood of Christ[36] regularly every Sunday. This in itself demands some explanation. How often did the nuns of Aywières go to Communion? We cannot say. If we consult the *Consuetudines* of Citeaux, the usages drawn up by our first Fathers, and which bound the nuns as well as the monks of the Order, we find that they urged what was then maximum frequency in the reception of the Holy Eucharist. Daily Communion was practically unknown. It was in the Middle Ages that annual Communion had to be made a law of the Church. The *Consuetudines* obliged Cistercians to go to Communion on Christmas Day, Holy Thursday, Easter, and Pentecost, and strongly advised them to go on every Sunday and important feast day throughout the year.[37] Those who were not able to receive our Lord in the Blessed Sacrament on Sundays were encouraged to do so during the week. Consequently, St.

---

[35] Ut autem aliquibus, quae minus forte digne de ea in Aquiria sentiebant, piae Lutgardis meritum monstraretur, . . . cum euntem ad altare nullus eam in subsidium debilis corporis sustentaret, manifeste viderunt aliquae . . . duos eam angelos mediam tenere (*Vita*, 203 b).

[36] All religious of the Cistercian Order received Communion under both species for many years after the practice was abandoned by the Church at large.

[37] *Consuetudines*, I, caput lx.

Lutgarde was only keeping the Rule. However, it must be admitted that Sunday Communion was a counsel, not an obligation, and so the fact that Communion was less frequent in many Flemish convents does not, in itself, prove that they were irregular, but only that they were infected with the same coldness that pervaded the whole Church and which was, in fact, a matter of custom and habit to which, perhaps more than anything else, may be ascribed the growth of heresies and schisms that finally tore so many regions and nations from the fold of the Church.

The truth is, that far from following the advice of St. Stephen Harding and his successors who drew up the *Consuetudines,* the nuns of our Flemish convents probably did not receive Communion more than six or seven times in the year. Frequency varied from convent to convent.[88] However, the mere fact that we know so much about the lack of interest in the Blessed Sacrament in the Low Countries at this time is due not to the fact that tepidity was there at its greatest but that, on the contrary, it was there that the reaction began, and developed in its fullest force. The Flemish mystics of the thirteenth century were the leaders of this revival of love for Jesus in the Blessed Sacrament, and it was Bl. Juliana of Mount Cornillon, outside Liége, who suffered persecution and exile, and struggled valiantly for years, almost singlehanded, against the opposition of secular and even ecclesiastical powers, to bring about the institution of the Feast of Corpus Christi. Bl. Juliana was, herself, an Augustinian nun, but when she fled from Mount Cornillon in a time of civil war she found refuge in the Cistercian community that was eventually to settle at Flines outside Douai, but which was then at Salzinnes, not far from Namur.

[88] At Roosendael, when Bl. Ida of Louvain entered there, the novices were *prohibited* from approaching the Blessed Sacrament more than three times in the year.

Christ in the Blessed Sacrament was the center of the interior life of the 13th century Cistercian mystics. We have mentioned Bl. Ida of Louvain and Bl. Ida of Léau, who were especially remarkable for their devotion to the Holy Eucharist. Ida of Louvain had many visions and revelations concerning this Sacrament of Christ's love.

Because of her devotion to the Sacred Heart and to the Passion of Christ, St. Lutgarde was inevitably drawn to the Blessed Sacrament which Christ instituted as a living memorial of His Passion. How could it be otherwise? The Holy Sacrifice of the Mass is not merely a symbolic representation of Calvary, it *is* Calvary, and Christ is mystically placed in a state of sacrifice on our altars in the separate consecration of bread and wine as His Body and Blood. When the whole Christian world had grown cold and indifferent to the meaning of this tremendous reality which lies at the very core of the whole economy of grace and salvation, and upon which, therefore, the whole happiness and well-being of the human race depends, a few poor nuns and a handful of uneducated recluses, hidden in their convents and cells, were living a life that was a vital and continuous awareness of the Real Presence of Jesus in the Host.

When thousands of bishops and priests had become so engrossed in matters of law, for the sake of defending their temporal interests, that they spent more time in the law courts than in the sanctuary, and could barely be persuaded to say Mass once a week, a few Flemish women were burning with love for the neglected and despised Christ whom they all but saw, crowned with thorns and clad in ignominy, in the plain, pale Host.

It was no coincidence that miracles like that of the bleeding Host preserved at Herkenrode began to occur at this time, and that God began to reveal Himself simultaneously to so many pure and hidden souls. The way was being prepared for the great theologian of the Holy Eucharist, St. Thomas Aquinas, who eventually composed the beautiful Office for the Feast of Corpus Christi, and some of the most solemn and stirring hymns to the Blessed Sacrament.

The frequent Communions of St. Lutgarde were still the exception, even in religion. She was ahead of her times — or behind them, if you prefer to look back to the Eucharistic fervor which was the strength of the early martyrs. And so, her sisters had not all received the grace to appreciate her awareness of the Real Presence and to understand how much the Blessed Sacrament really meant to her. They believed in the Real Presence, no doubt: but they had never *experienced* it. On appropriate occasions they went piously and dutifully to Communion, and said a few extra prayers afterward. But it never occurred to them all that time that Christ was really, physically entering into the very depths of their being. So far as their affections were concerned, He might as well have remained in the remotest heights of heaven: He was not real to them — or if He was, the reality was clouded with confusion and embarrassment and fear. Familiar and confident love became impossible. Instead of loving Holy Communion, they kept away.

When such souls saw how Mother Lutgarde continued to defy the established custom and to reproach their own coldness by her frequent Communions, they naturally resented it and began to criticize her. No doubt they were perfectly sincere. They did not know any better. They had never seen such a thing before. It could only appear to them to be presumption. They probably thought that the saint was deluded and eccentric: or that she was putting on airs, trying to be superior, making herself better than everybody else.

So they went to the abbess of the convent, Mother Agnes, and complained of St. Lutgarde's Sunday Communions. Thomas does not tell us that Lutgarde's superioress acted out

of any unworthy motive, but she evidently shared the prejudices of the sisters, and considered it her duty to forbid the
saint to receive Communion so frequently.

What follows must be told cautiously, lest anyone gather
the impression that St. Lutgarde and the powers of heaven
connived together in a kind of preternatural vendetta against
the abbess. Nevertheless, it was a punishment. But Lutgarde
had nothing to do with it, apart from being its occasion.

When she received orders from her mother abbess to
abstain from weekly Communion, St. Lutgarde sorrowfully
but humbly replied: "I will obey you with all my heart,
Reverend Mother, but there is one thing I must tell you.
It is this. I can foretell that, in all truth, Christ will take
vengeance for this injury against Him, upon your flesh."

Almost immediately after this, the mother superioress of
Aywières was afflicted with a severe illness which kept her
out of the church altogether, and which became more and
more painful from moment to moment, until she lifted the
ban she had imposed upon the saint's Communions. Then
she got better. Several others who were opposed to the saint,
either suffered calamities of their own or changed their opinion
of her ways. P. Jonquet[39] compares this incident in the life
of St. Lutgarde to that of her remote successor, who was
to become the most famous propagator of devotion to the
Sacred Heart. St. Margaret Mary had been forbidden, in
much the same way, to practice the "Holy Hour" which had
been enjoined upon her by our Lord Himself, and the mother
superioress of Paray received what she considered a warning
from God in the sudden and very peculiar death of one of
her best subjects. However, it must be repeated that in
neither case were these calamities desired by either of the
saints concerned, who resigned themselves in simple obedience
to the will of their superiors. However, when God has some

[39] *Ste. Lutgarde, la Marguerite Marie Belge*, p. 108.

special end in view, in which the salvation of many souls is concerned, He can and occasionally does manifest His will by signs of this nature. But it is not His usual way.

If some of St. Lutgarde's sisters were piqued by the extraordinary favors she received in prayer, they must have had a bad moment on the day when she became so fervent in choir that a flame was seen to shoot out of her mouth and ascend into the air. A young nun, who happened to look up just in time to catch sight of this strange phenomenon, was so panic stricken that she fell over in a dead faint. What is most interesting about this story is the fact that these things did not make St. Lutgarde vain. She explained why, to Thomas of Cantimpré, in terms that invite reflection. She said that she was, on such occasions, so filled with true and solid spiritual glory from within, that no vainglory from without could seriously tempt her: and the Holy Spirit supported her like an immovable column.[40]

St. Lutgarde's explanation of her immunity from vainglory would seem to imply that the external manifestation of the interior grace meant practically nothing to her. It was something which, so far as her own sanctity was concerned, was completely indifferent, and she only took pleasure in it so far as it might give some accidental glory to God. She evidently did not bother to try to find out just exactly how it did so: God could take care of that. But what precisely did she mean by solid, spiritual glory that filled her from within? It was the Word living in her, for He is the splendor of the glory of the Father, "and the figure of His substance, and upholding all things by the word of His power, making purgation of sins."[41]

Such, at least, is the teaching of St. Bernard, who points

----

[40] Adeo spirituali et solida interius gloria plena fuit, quod nulla eam forinsecus inanis gloria vexare potuit: sed veluti columnam Spiritus sanctus eam immobilem fixit (*Vita*, 200 a).

[41] Hebr. 1:2.

out how intimately present God is to the soul — so intimately that He Himself is the light of the soul and its strength and, ultimately, its glory: not formally and substantially, but causally,[42] granting the soul, by His free gift, participation in His divine nature.

This story shows the importance of the liturgy, especially of the Divine Office, in the spirituality of St. Lutgarde. We have seen how the graces of the liturgy operated in her more or less independently of her understanding of the meaning of the words she was singing: a truth that ought to be consoling not only to those religious, and especially novices, who do not know much Latin, but also to those who, no matter how earnestly and sincerely they try, are unable to fix their attention for any length of time upon the actual words before them in the book, and who are also in a state in which meditation on any theme, however general, is practically out of the question.

If God gives such extraordinary manifestations of His presence in a soul during the Divine Office, it is not merely in order to provide diversion for those who happen to be present, and excite them, for the time being, to more fervent praise of Him. He desires that we should know, by this means, how much He is pleased with the chanting of the Office, even by the unlettered and the simple.

We have seen how the saint was raised up into the air while singing the *Veni Creator Spiritus*. Another magnificent hymn, the *Te Deum*, was the occasion of signal mystical graces. At the verse: *Tu ad liberandum suscepturus hominem non horruisti Virginis uterum* ("When Thou didst come to deliver man, Thou didst not abhor the Virgin's womb") St. Lutgarde once saw our Lady appear, radiant with joy and glory. Thomas of Cantimpré adds that St. Lutgarde frequently received similar lights and favors during the singing of the

---

[42] *Sermons on the Canticle of Canticles, iv, 4.*

psalms.[43] Incidentally, the apparition of our Lady during the *Te Deum* reminds us that St. Lutgarde was not entirely ignorant of everything that was sung: she understood the meaning of this particular line, at any rate.

So, too, she followed the Gospels of the Mass with intelligent attention and with a most particular devotion, as we can readily understand, knowing the spirit of faith with which she saw and heard Christ Himself speaking to her as the words were sung. Five years before her death, during the singing of the Gospel of the Third Sunday after Pentecost, she learned, by revelation, that she would die on that day. The revelation sprang, so to speak, from the Gospel itself, which, according to the ancient Cistercian missal was that of the "Man who made a great supper and invited many" (Luke 14:16).

It was revealed to her, then, that she herself would enter into the eternal banquet, the wedding feast of heaven on this day. She told Sybil de Gages about it. She usually told these visions to Mother Sybil, who knew Latin, to find out whether or not the revelation fitted the text. Sybil evidently gave her approval, but then forgot all about the affair, until five years later. When the saint was laid out for burial the same Gospel was sung and her friend remembered the prophecy.[44]

St. Lutgarde's mysticism was a constant vital expression of the liturgical cycle, and visions on the feasts of the saints and of the time testify to her profoundly intelligent and affective awareness of the meaning of the different seasons of the ecclesiastical year, and her full participation in the graces of each one. This is a fact which cannot be overstressed, when we are talking about monastic spirituality. The chief work of the Benedictine and Cistercian is to praise God in choir, in the harmonious daily round of offices that wheels about the cen-

[43] *Vita*, 202 a.
[44] *Vita*, 205 e.

tral hub of the Conventual Mass. There are, therefore, two reasons in particular why the liturgy should be by far the most fruitful source of graces, and should be the most effective means for arriving at the highest degree of contemplation and union with God. The first of these is that if God willed St. Benedict to establish a contemplative Order, and willed that the chief means of contemplation prescribed by its Rule should be the Divine Office, the *Opus Dei,* to which "nothing is to be preferred,"[45] it must follow that God intended normally to mete out graces of prayer and union to His servants through the liturgy. The second reason is that since the Office is part of an integral whole of which the core and marrow is the Sacrifice of the Mass, all the canonical hours are channels through which the graces and benefits of Christ's redeeming Sacrifice are communicated in a special way to the souls of those who participate in the chanting, as well as to the Church at large through them.

Devotion to the Incarnation of the Word necessarily means devotion to His Virgin Mother. The Cistercians grew up in the twelfth century, and their influence dominated the age when the great cathedrals of Europe were being built or rebuilt with a perfection that bore witness to the deepest and most powerful aspirations in the souls of men. In the doors of these cathedrals stood the statue of the Mother of God, holding the infant Christ in her arms. This taught the faithful that she was the gate of heaven — *janua coeli* — she was the cause of our joy, the Mother of all grace: that no one came to Jesus save through her.

St. Bernard and Bl. Guerric and many other Cistercian doctors insisted on the doctrine of Mary, Mediatrix of all grace, and when St. Bernard was able to *choose for himself* a subject on which to write, it was a series of sermons on the

---

[45] "Nihil operi Dei praeponatur," Reg. S. Bened., c. 43.

Mystery of the Incarnation, the homilies on the *"Missus Est."* That meant, of course, simply a series of sermons in praise of the Virgin Mother of Christ.

Cistercian mysticism centers upon the Word of God, through whom we come to the Father. And the Word comes to us Incarnate. Jesus is the Word of God. And Jesus comes to us only in the arms of His Virgin Mother, eternally generated from His Father's substance, in the Godhead, but born in time from the substance of His Mother as Man. Therefore, the Virgin Mother, holding in her arms the divine Child, is the key to Cistercian mysticism as she is, indeed, to Christian spirituality. Truly she is the "gate of heaven."

The true Cistercian is always at least virtually aware of his particularly close relation to our Lady. His white cowl is the special livery of her service.[46] It reminds him always that he belongs entirely, body and soul, to Mary. He tends to live very much in her presence, that is to say, in a habitual awareness of the real personal interest which keeps her concerned with all that he does, as she intercedes before the throne of God with special urgency and efficacy for her chosen sons, her Cistercian knights, her shock troops, men living only for the glory of her Son. More than that, the monk is guided in all that he does by her will, her love, her influence.

This extraordinary union with Mary reached such a pitch in the life of St. Lutgarde that, for five years, she was visited by the Queen of Heaven in vision almost every day: and if Mary did not come to her, Lutgarde saw one of the saints. So far as the latter are concerned, St. Lutgarde's visions are fairly representative of the devotions common in the Order

---

[46] A legend — the origin of which is not very certain — ascribes to our Lady's special intervention, the choice of white as the color of the Cistercian cowl by St. Alberic. If this is not recorded in any of the ancient documents of our Fathers, nevertheless the *Exordium Magnum,* a twelfth-century collection of legends of our Order, testifies to the extraordinary devotion of the early Cistercians to the Mother of God — a devotion never equaled in the Church before their time (Migne, *P. L.,* vol. 185).

in the Middle Ages. It is interesting to see how times have changed.

In the twelfth and thirteenth centuries, on some of the great feasts of the sanctoral cycle, there were not only two Masses, as we have them in our Cistercian monasteries today, but *two distinct proper Masses* for the saint of the day, both to be said, at specified times, on the day of his feast.

So, for instance, on the Feasts of SS. Peter and Paul and of St. John the Baptist's Nativity, the Matutinal Mass of the day differed from the Major Mass, having proper Introit, Epistle, and so on: but both Masses were for the saint. In our own day, of course, the Matutinal Mass sometimes differs from the Major Mass, but only in order to commemorate some *other* feast.

It would be hard to exaggerate the importance of St. John the Baptist to the early Cistercians. As far back as St. Benedict, and indeed as the Thebaid, St. John Baptist was regarded as the pattern and patron of monks, and we know that St. Benedict dedicated chapels to him and to St. Martin of Tours on Monte Cassino, after overthrowing the altars of pagan deities there. The piety of our own day is, as a whole, not attracted to the austere Precursor: he is not thought to exercise a sufficient appeal to the heart. But that is far from being true: the thing that most recommends St. John the Baptist to the contemplation of the Cistercian monk or nun is that he really is a model of the love of Christ, a love which is summed up, not in flowery prayers or in pretty sentiments, but in the exultant cry: "He must increase, and I must decrease!"

Devotion to the Precursor misses its mark unless it grasps the one essential truth of his vocation which was, not merely to live on locusts and wild honey in the desert, not merely to preach penance to the Jews, but to proclaim Christ and then vanish from the scene. The Christocentrism of Cistercian spirituality seized upon this one fact: and there is no cause for wonder that the monks of our Order have always found contemplation of this magnificent love a source of grace and an explanation of our whole vocation to the solitary life.

The Gospels tell us how the Precursor summed up his own vocation and ours: "He that hath the bride, is the Bridegroom: but the friend of the Bridegroom, who standeth and heareth him, rejoiceth with joy because of the Bridegroom's voice. *This my joy therefore is fulfilled. He must increase, I must decrease.*"[47]

St. Lutgarde also had great devotion to the child-martyr, St. Agnes. It is easy to see why. A glance at the Office of St. Agnes' feast shows us the full and complete flowering of the language of the Mystical Espousals and the Mystical Marriage with Christ: and this is not due to the mere fancy of some liturgist. We know that the ancient liturgical Offices were not usually drawn simply out of the imagination, but woven together about definite scriptural themes, or, in the case of a saint, made up of a mosaic of passages from his original biography, or from the acts of his martyrdom.

Now, as a matter of fact, the first and second nocturns of the Feast of St. Agnes in the old Cistercian Breviary are drawn from St. Ambrose's account of her passion, upon which are also based most of the responsories and antiphons that have survived even in the present Office. The words of St. Ambrose show us conclusively that St. Agnes was a mystic who had little to learn even from St. Teresa or St. John of the Cross. The doctrine of the great Carmelites and even much of their terminology seems to have been already realized centuries before in the interior life of the little Roman martyr.

The accusation brought against Agnes by the father of her rejected suitor, and to which one of her servants bore witness, was "that she had been a Christian from her earliest child-

47 John 3:29–31.

hood, and was so engrossed in the arts of magic that she said that Christ was her Spouse."[48]

The Office of the saint in the present Cistercian Breviary gives sufficient indication of the depth of her interior life, since the strange and beautiful antiphons and responsories are mostly quotations from the statements she made about her union with Christ.

"I have received milk and honey from His mouth, and His Blood shows in the redness of my cheeks."[49] "I am espoused to Him whom the angels serve, and upon whose beauty the sun and moon are ever gazing."[50] "The Lord has clad me in a garment woven of gold, and has bedecked me with immense jewels."[51] "I love Christ, and I have entered into His bridal chamber: whose Mother is a Virgin, and whose Father knows no woman: and, when I shall have loved Him, I shall be chaste: and when I shall have touched Him, I shall be clean, and when I shall have received Him to me, I shall be a virgin indeed!"[52]

Such statements from a thirteen-year-old girl are clear evidence of the heights of transforming union, and show that she had entered in boldly before the very throne of God and had drunk from the same springs of eternal truth as St. John the Evangelist and St. Paul. They bear witness to the experience of a union with God so close and intimate and so

[48] Old Cistercian Brev., *In Festo S. Agnetis*, II Noct., Lectio 8.

[49] Mel et lac ex ore ejus suscepi, et sanguis ejus ornavit genas meas (i Noct., ant. 5).

[50] Ipsi sum desponsata cui angeli serviunt, cujus pulcritudinem sol et luna mirantur (ii Noct., ant. 3).

[51] Induit me Dominus cyclade auro texta, et immensis monilibus ornavit me (i Noct., ant. 4).

[52] Amo Christum, in cujus thalamum introivi: cujus mater virgo est, cujus Pater foeminam nescit. . . . Quem cum amavero casta sum, cum tetigero munda sum, cum accepero, virgo sum (from the 3rd Resp., i Noct.). The references to these antiphons and responsory, as well as to the lesson quoted above, are taken from an old Spanish Cistercian Breviary, printed in 1595 at Salamanca.

perfectly consummated, that His life had become the life of her soul, and His attributes had worked in her to purify her of all sin, and to embellish her soul with the perfection of all the virtues — the "immense jewels" to which she refers in her lovely, extravagant enthusiasm.

Now, anyone who is devoted to St. Agnes and has paid attention to her Office in the Breviary, whether Roman or Cistercian, probably has already noticed the fact that Thomas of Cantimpré, describing St. Lutgarde's vision of Christ and her consequent rejection of her earthly suitor, in her first days at St. Catherine's, placed in her mouth the very words which Ambrose attributes to St. Agnes. *Discede a me, pabulum mortis*, "Get away from me, thou bait of death, thou food of crime: I already belong to another Lover."[53]

There is no need to try to settle the question whether St. Lutgarde herself had spontaneously used the words from the Office of St. Agnes, or whether Thomas merely takes the liberty of attributing them to her in order to drive home a point which is one of the minor themes of the *Vita*: that St. Lutgarde was a second Agnes. The question cannot really be settled. But there is no doubt of the importance of this theme to Thomas of Cantimpré. The parallel between the two saints is something which assumed considerable importance in his eyes. One might argue that this might naturally be expected to occur to him, because of the external similarity of the situations in which the two girls were placed, and in which they showed their preference for Christ over all earthly lovers. Both were about the same age at the time of their trial. But

---

[53] St. Agnes got rid of her rich suitor with the words: Discede a me, fomes peccati, nutrimentum facinoris, pabulum mortis. Discede a me, quia jam ab alio amatore praeventa sum . . . et annulo fidei suae subarravit me longe te nobilior, et genere et dignitate (Old Cist. Brev., i Noct., Lect. 4). — "Depart from me, thou fomentor of sins, thou food of crime, thou bait of death. Depart from me, for I already belong to another Lover . . . who has espoused me with the ring of His faith, and who is of far nobler birth than thou, of better blood and high above thee in dignity."

the resemblance goes deeper than this, and, in any case, it was not Thomas of Cantimpré's own idea at all.

When St. Lutgarde was just entering into the secret realms of mystical knowledge of Christ, a woman, seeing her in ecstasy, was herself filled with a kind of spirit of prophecy, and cried out: "As I see, thou art a good Agnes, and truly, thou shalt be a second Agnes."[54] Thomas saw the fulfillment of this prophecy in the stigmatization of St. Lutgarde.

Everyone knows more or less what stigmatization is. The story of St. Francis meditating on the Passion of Christ, alone on a mountain, and suddenly seeing a winged seraph in the air before him, with the figure of the crucified Christ set in the midst of those flaming wings, and receiving from the wounds of the Christ in the seraph wounds in his own hands and feet and side — all this is familiar, at least to Catholics. The case of the stigmatized Theresa Neumann in our own time is also a famous one, and indeed one of the fortunate accidents of World War II was the fact that many American Catholic soldiers got to see her with their own eyes.

We do not need to enter upon a discussion of the possibility of such a thing. Medical science has never been able to work out a natural explanation for genuine stigmatization — and if it had, be sure that everyone would have heard all about it long ago! The vague, disgruntled accusations of hysteria leveled against stigmatics have never had much effect, because it has been almost impossible, even for a prejudiced judge, to decide conclusively that any real stigmatic showed symptoms of hysteria. On the other hand, hysterics and maniacs who have produced these wounds in themselves, or in whom the stigmalike manifestations have occurred in connection with some abnormal pathological condition, have never manifested the perfection and

[54] Tu, ut video, bona Agnes; et vere Agnes altera eris (*Vita*, 192 a).

regularity of the appearing and disappearing wounds of true stigmatics. Stigmatized saints have, often for years, been afflicted with extremely painful, regularly recurring wounds in the hands and feet, which emit blood copiously for several hours at a time, which cannot be healed by any ordinary means, and which, nevertheless, disappear quite suddenly, sometimes without a trace, only to recur in due time. These wounds are generally accompanied by ecstasies and often by other clearly supernatural manifestations. Finally, one must take into account the heroic virtues, patience, meekness, and charity of the true stigmatic.

On the other hand, doctors and hypnotists and psychoanalysts have been working hard, with much concentration and intensity of purpose, in an effort to prove that the stigmata can be produced by natural means — by hypnotism and autosuggestion. Their efforts have never produced anything but a slight discoloration of the skin, or at most a barely visible ooze of blood through the pores.

Catholic pathologists have entered into profound studies on the subject, some of them in an effort to prove that stigmata might be the effect of an extraordinarily active imagination upsetting the body. Poulain even quotes St. Francis de Sales in a passage where the great Bishop of Geneva maintains that, in the stigmatization of St. Francis, the imagination exercised an important role in transmitting the pains of the wounds to their proper places in the hands and feet, but he adds that the wounds themselves could not be produced by the work of the imagination alone.[55]

The best theological explanation of the stigmata is given by St. John of the Cross: but in quoting it we warn the reader that this is not being offered as a medical or psycho-

---

[55] *Treatise on the Love of God,* Book VI, chap. 15. We refer the reader to Poulain, *Graces of Interior Prayer,* xxxi, No. 8 ff., for a complete discussion of stigmatization.

logical proof, and it presupposes enough familiarity with scholastic metaphysics to admit the existence of pure spirits, capable of acting as God's intermediaries in this work.

Stigmata, for St. John of the Cross, are simply external wounds which sometimes accompany and manifest interior wounds, produced in the simple and immaterial soul, by the powerful, mystical action of infused love. Sometimes these burning wounds, or "cauteries" are produced by direct contact with the very substance of God, and sometimes they are the result of the action of a "seraph" with a "flaming dart." It should not be necessary to point out that the "flaming dart" is nothing material or visible. The language in which St. John of the Cross described this wounding of the soul by love is purely symbolical, but that does not mean that what it expresses is not a real experience: on the contrary, it is evident that his symbols fall far short of the reality.

He tells us how the soul, like a white-hot "furnace" of love, is visited by a seraph, who pierces its substance, transverberating it with this "fiery dart," so that a wild flame leaps from the soul, and the wound left by the dart begins to spread and to invade the whole soul with pain and delight. Then, in the midst of this wound thus produced, a tiny, but fiercely active grain of fire, which the saint calls a grain of mustard seed, begins to pour forth spirals of blazing love that soon fill and occupy the entire extent of the soul in all its ramifications and faculties, until it seems to be swimming in an ocean of delight and of pure love.

St. John of the Cross, then, having described the important thing, the interior cautery of infused love, goes on to say that occasionally this is accompanied by exterior wounds in the flesh. He cites St. Francis of Assisi and, what is more, St. Paul, interpreting in this sense "I bear the marks of the Lord Jesus in my body."[56]

[56] Gal. 6:17. St. John of the Cross, *The Living Flame of Love*, II, 2.

Enough of this general discussion. What about St. Lutgarde? One of the most interesting facts about her stigmatization was that it had an intimate connection with her devotion to St. Agnes.

St. Lutgarde had a tremendous desire to prove her love for Christ by suffering martyrdom for His sake. This was nothing merely Platonic in her soul. It was more than the lively affections following upon the work of an ardent fancy: it was a true mystical grace. And the desire was so strong that, in itself, it was a real interior and mystical martyrdom for her.

One night, then, she had gone to the dormitory and was praying by her bed before retiring, when the thought of martyrdom came to her. She remembered St. Agnes, and was filled with so powerful and so burning a desire to die for Christ, like the Roman virgin martyr, that the might of her love became almost strong enough to kill her outright. Then suddenly a vein near her heart burst, and through a wide open wound in her side, blood began to pour forth, soaking her robe and cowl. As she lost her senses and sank to the floor, Christ appeared to her, in glory, His face radiant with joy, and said to her:

"Because of the great and fervent desire of martyrdom with which thou hast now shed thy blood, know that thou shalt receive the same reward in heaven as the most blessed Agnes received, in the severing of her head for My faith: because by thy desire even unto the shedding of blood, thou hast equaled her martyrdom."[57]

Thus wounded once, with a wound like the spear wound in Christ's Heart, Lutgarde was never wounded again: but she kept the scar until the end of her life. This occurred in her twenty-ninth year.

[57] Pro desideratissimo fervore martyrii, quem in effusione istius sanguinis habuisti, idem martyrii meritum in coelo recipies, quod Agnes beatissima, profide mea in capitis abscissione suscepit: quia martyrium ejus in tuo desiderio in sanguine compensasti (*Vita,* 200 e).

However, on many occasions in her life as a Cistercian, in meditating on Christ's Passion, she would fall into an ecstasy, and a sweat of blood would begin to cover her body as she participated, to some degree, in His interior sufferings.[58]

A priest who heard of this watched for an opportunity to verify it with his own eyes. He waited until a time when the saint could usually be found on her knees in adoration, and went to the church. Sure enough, he found her in ecstasy, leaning against the wall, her face and hands dripping with blood. The curious priest went up to her full of the spirit of scientific investigation and armed with a pair of scissors. With these he cut off a lock of the saint's hair, by which we may conclude that his love of science was greater than his good manners. As he stood marveling at the drops of blood on the lock in his hand, St. Lutgarde came to herself, and then, instantly, the drops of blood vanished, not only from her face and hands, but, at the same time, from the lock of hair in the priest's hand. At this, the investigator was so taken aback that he nearly collapsed.[59]

Witnesses of the stigmatization of St. Lutgarde's side were two nuns, one called Margaret, the other Lutgarde of Limmos, who washed the saint's clothes.

There is no need, after this, to repeat that the center of St. Lutgarde's interior life was the Passion of Christ. Devotion to the Sacred Heart means devotion to Christ's infinite love for men: and the two greatest proofs and pledges of that love are the cross and the Holy Eucharist. It may be possible for some of us today to separate these two in our devotions: but if we do

---

[58] St. Gemma Galgani, in our own century, frequently suffered the same thing. The mere sound of blasphemies used to make her sweat blood.

[59] *Vita*, 201 a. Incidentally Thomas of Cantimpré's explanation of this sweat of blood comes close to the opinion of St. Francis de Sales quoted above. He says: " . . . ex intellectuali consideratione mentis interius similitudinem traxit corpus exterius." In other words, the influence of her ecstatic soul was the proximate cause of the bloody sweat on her body.

so, we are to that extent lacking in Catholicity. After all, the Mass is Calvary. The Blessed Sacrament loses much of its meaning as soon as it ceases to be conscious participation in Christ's sacrifice and a memorial of the Passion. True, we may profitably emphasize upon occasion the fact that by this Sacrament Christ is present with us in the tabernacle: but the love that this presence implies and demands is not sufficiently understood if we forget that this Christ is not only God and Man, but suffered, was crucified, and died for us, and rose again from the dead. He has left us this Sacrament as a pledge of His triumph: but His triumph is enacted before us each day on our altars at Mass.

St. Thomas explains that the Eucharist produces in man the same effect as the Passion: sanctifying grace.[60]

When the Cistercian Fathers spoke of Spiritual Communion, they meant something more than a spiritual reception of the Eucharist made possible by an act of desire proceeding from a lively faith. For them the notion of Communion was intimately connected with that of the Sacrifice of Calvary. And when the first Cistercians practiced this devotion, they did not merely recollect themselves and inwardly express a desire to receive that Sacrament spiritually, and to have Jesus present spiritually within them. Spiritual Communion was for them the *Res Sacramenti*, the real essence of Communion, the object one should have in view in all Communions, whether sacramental or, according to our term, "spiritual." And for them this fruit *was to share in the Passion of Christ*. Nor did they restrict this sharing merely to participation in the merits and consolations derived from the Passion: for them, spiritual Communion, that is, real Communion, meant sharing in both the fruits of the Passion, and *in its sufferings*. By this, of course, they meant

[60] Per hoc sacramentum repraesentatur Passio Christi: ideo effectum quem Passio Christi fecit in mundo, hoc sacramentum facit in homine (*Summa Theol.*, III, q. 79, a1).

following Christ on the Way of the Cross, living a life of mortification, self-denial, and accepting all the trials sent to them by Christ for this very purpose of allowing them the intimacy of this "spiritual Communion." Hence when they made "spiritual Communion" they always renewed their offering of themselves with Christ as victims.

Thus, in a certain sense, our Fathers considered the whole Cistercian life as a spiritual Communion because their whole life was a Mass, a sacrifice. St. Aelred of Rievaulx, when he speaks of the active and passive purifications of our contemplative life, frequently brings out this particular purpose underlying all our trials. He compares those who shrink from the difficulties and sufferings of that period of spiritual dryness which follows the consolations of beginners, to those who were scandalized by our Lord's first revelation of the Eucharist. Those who give up their spiritual exercises as hopeless as soon as they are afflicted with aridity and deprived of consolations reminded St. Aelred of the disciples who, when Jesus told them they would eat the flesh of the Son of Man, and drink His Blood, murmured that "this saying is hard, and who can hear it?" and "went back, and walked no more with Him."[61] The reason the saint gives for his opinion is that those monks who refuse to accept any trial or bear with any repugnance by that very fact refuse "Communion in the Body and Blood of the Lord, that is to say, the imitation of His Passion."[62] Therefore, we see that St. Aelred explicitly identifies the *glad acceptance of sufferings and trials* with spiritual Communion because this implies our union with Christ the Victim in the Mass.

William of St. Thierry, in his "Epistle to the Brethren of

[61] See St. John, Chap. vi, 48–72.
[62] Communicationem Dominici Corporis et Sanguinis, id est passionis illius imitationem abhorrent, dicentes "durus est hic sermo" (St. Aelred, *Speculum Charitatis*, ii, 13).

Mont-Dieu"[63] describes "spiritual Communion" simply as recalling to mind Christ's Passion, and dwelling lovingly and
thoughtfully upon everything that it means. To do this is to
eat Christ's flesh and drink His blood, in a spiritual manner.

There is no need to go any further. This is quite sufficient
to show that St. Lutgarde was a perfect example of Cistercian
devotion to the Mass, to the Blessed Sacrament and to the
Sacred Heart. All were summed up, for her, in a consuming
love for the Passion and death of our Saviour Jesus Christ.

Calvary was something she always contemplated, and which
she was ever striving to imitate, in order thus to prove her
love for Christ on the cross, and to be most perfectly united
to Him in this great Sacrifice, the greatest of all acts of love.

As a reward for her fervent and selfless love, she was
granted the special favors we have mentioned, and these, in
turn, enabled her to enter more fully into her participation
in Christ's sufferings and His immense love for His Father
and for unhappy sinners. As the years went by, and as her
desire for death and suffering grew stronger with each day,
Christ did not deny her the opportunities she desired. Bur-
dened with many exterior and interior crosses, broken with
sickness, she was finally visited with a terrible trial.

Eleven years before she died she became stone blind.

---

[63] Scit enim quicumque sensum Christi habet quantum pietati christianae
expediat . . . una saltem diei hora passionis et redemptionis ipsius attentius
recolere beneficia, ad fruendum suaviter in conscientia, et recondendum
fideliter in memoria, quod est spiritualiter manducare corpus Christi et
bibere ejus sanguinem in memoriam ejus qui omnibus in se credentibus
praecepit dicens: "Hoc facite in meam commemorationem" (*Ep. ad Fratres
de Monte Dei,* i, 10, No. 30).

"Anyone who has the true Christian sense knows how valuable an aid
to Christian piety is the practice of recalling to mind, with a more
especial attention, for at least one hour of the day, the benefits of the
Passion and Redemption, in order to dwell with loving joy upon them
in one's mind, and to store them away faithfully in the memory. To do
this, is to spiritually eat the Body of Christ and to drink His Blood, in
memory of Him who gave, as a precept, to all those believing in Him,
that they should 'do this in memory of Me.'"

CHAPTER SEVEN

ST. LUTGARDE'S SCHOOL OF MYSTICISM AT AYWIÈRES. HER RELATIONS WITH THE ORDER OF PREACHERS

THOMAS OF CANTIMPRÉ nowhere goes into detail about St. Lutgarde's many sicknesses. He barely tells us in a general way that she had them. And, as a matter of fact, the weird terminology of medieval medicine would not help us much, even if he had decided to be a little more graphic. We have no notion why or how St. Lutgarde went blind. He merely throws out a casual remark that she did not find it cost so much to be deprived of the sight of earthly things, since she was constantly refreshed, inwardly, by the abundant illuminations of divine charismata, and rested peacefully in intimate union with the Spouse of her soul.

Nevertheless, if there was one thing that did cause her a little sorrow, it was the fact that she was no longer able to enjoy the sight of her spiritual friends.[1]

Far from being jealous, and far from punishing her for this, Christ sympathized with her, and assured her, in return for the sacrifice, that if she patiently bore with her affliction she would not only escape all punishment in purgatory, but would speedily be united with all her friends in heaven. Here we have two concepts which may mildly surprise many religious —and lay persons— of our own day.[2]

[1] Hoc solum pia Lutgardis in hac caecitate plangebat, quod spirituales amicos suos in hac vita ulterius non videret (*Vita*, 204 d).
[2] *Ibidem.*

The first of these is, of course, the mere suggestion that someone who had suffered as much as St. Lutgarde, made so many sacrifices, and lived so holy a life, should have to pass through purgatory.

In the present day there are some who seem to think that purgatory is not to be feared, and that a few acts of love will suffice to wash away all our sins and imperfections, thus enabling us to go straight to heaven after death. What is the basis of this somewhat hazy doctrine? To what sources is it to be traced? Perhaps it has arisen from a misinterpretation of the spirituality of the Little Flower. If so, a closer examination of the writings of St. Thérèse will show that a quick entry into heaven is, indeed, promised to those who follow the "Little Way," but the Little Way consists in more than *formulating* acts of love and in *declaring* oneself to be perfectly abandoned to the merciful love of God. As a matter of fact, the uncompromising heroism demanded by the complete and utter exspoliation of self-will and of one's own judgment, the total humility, the uncompromising obedience to God's slightest desire and the utterly blind confidence in Him which the Little Way prescribes should do much to purify the soul of all the imperfections inherent in our fallen nature. But the Little Way must be followed, not merely admired, and it is to be feared that the doctrine of the Little Flower has more admirers than imitators.

The teaching of St. Bernard, and of St. John of the Cross, and of the Church as a whole, including St. Thérèse, for that matter, is that we cannot enter into perfect union of love with God in heaven until our souls have been completely stripped of everything that is in the slightest degree opposed to the purity and sanctity of His will. This does not merely mean that we have to repent of our sins and resolve not to commit them any more: we must do penance, offer satisfaction for them. And, once again, whether we look to St. Bernard,

St. John of the Cross, the Little Flower, or any other mystical doctor in the Church, they are unhesitating and unanimous in declaring that the only perfect way of offering God this satisfaction and of purifying our souls is by love: and not only by doing everything that is within our own power to show our love for Him, but, even more, by allowing Him free scope to work upon our souls, directly by His own power or indirectly through the intermediary of persons and events, to complete this work of purification.

We have taken away something from God by sin: we have taken away the likeness of His own image, which He created in our souls. Christ, in His infinitely merciful love, has made it possible for us, by grace, to give back to God something of what we have taken from Him. What can we give Him? One thing only. St. Bernard tells us what it is: love. And, make no mistake: St. Bernard insists that, although our love cannot please God unless it is supernaturalized by grace, nevertheless, the love we give Him is *our* love — we alone can give it to Him. If we do not give Him our hearts He will never have them, for, precisely, to love Him is to give Him our free wills, and give them freely.

"Love," he says, "is the only one of all the movements and affections of the soul with which a creature, although not to an equal degree, can repay his Creator in kind. . . . If He rules me, I must serve Him; if He commands me, I must obey Him. I cannot turn around and ask *Him* to serve *me,* ask *Him* to obey *me.* And yet, consider how different it is with love. For when God loves, He wants nothing else but to be loved in return: *the only reason why He loves is in order to be loved, because He knows that those who love Him will be made perfectly happy by their very love itself.*"[3]

[3] Solus est amor ex omnibus animae motibus vel affectibus, in quo potest creatura, etsi non ex aequo, respondere auctori, vel de simili mutuam rependere vicem. . . . Si dominatur me, oportet servire; si imperat, me oportet parere, et non vicissim a Deo vel servitium exigere, vel obsequium.

How profound and beautiful is the doctrine of the great Cistercian! He saw how God had created the human soul free, and, by that very fact, given it the capacity to love Him. He saw, moreover, how God had elevated man's freedom to the supernatural level by grace, and so to speak multiplied and reinforced his power to love. And why? Because love is the very nature of God Himself, and by loving, man would come to share in that divine nature, and live that divine life. Love itself would be the soul's everlasting beatitude, and it would desire and seek nothing else. Merely by loving, we can pay all our debts, and please God perfectly.

"Hoc sponsa abundat, hoc sponsus est contentus." "The bride has plenty of love, and love is all that the Bridegroom wants of her. He desires nothing else, and she has nothing else to give."[4]

From this, then, it is clear that there is nothing that God so much desires as to give souls opportunities of loving Him more and more perfectly in this life: the chief reason being, to repeat St. Bernard's statement, in order to give them the blessedness, the pure and perfect joy which can only be had by loving Him. He wants them to love, because love is their salvation, love is participation in His own infinite bliss.

But since true love involves the gift of their free will, the gift of themselves, God multiplies occasions and opportunities for souls to renounce their own wills, and to make this gift of themselves by love to Him. He is constantly busy, trying to persuade souls to accept the sufferings and trials and difficulties of life that will enable them to make this gift, that will teach them to learn what love is, ever more and more perfectly.

Nunc jam videas de amore quam aliter sit. Nam cum amat Deus, non aliud vult quam amari: quippe non ad aliud amat nisi ut ametur, sciens ipso amore beatos qui se amaverint (*Serm.* 83, *In Cantica,* Migne, 183, 1183).

[4] *Ibidem.*

This is why, after St. Lutgarde had served Him for years, God sent her heavier crosses than ever before, and added to all her interior and exterior trials the frightful affliction of blindness. The prudence of the world cannot understand this. Like Job's friends, the wise men of this earth shake their heads in disapproval. They cannot understand why suffering can have anything to do with love, because love, in their definition, means not *giving*, but *taking; having*, not *sacrificing*. And that is why, in the end, they are cheated and deceived: for, as is implicit in the quotation from St. Bernard, all that we *have* is our capacity to *give*: the only thing that is ours is our own free will. But that free will, as Christ Himself has warned us, is the seed that must be buried in the ground and die, or itself remaineth alone:[5] and if we take this, our single talent, and hide it away in a napkin until our Master come to claim it again, we shall be found at the last day with nothing at all.

Some, too, may be surprised that one so perfect as this saint should have complained that she could no longer enjoy the sight of her friends. They will ask: was this not an imperfection? Are saints supposed to have *friends?* This springs from another confusion. A soul that truly loves God fears merely "sentimental friendships" more than a disease: and, indeed, such things are a disease of the soul, in one dedicated entirely to God. They imply a division in our affections, a compromise. It would be a living lie for one who has given her heart to God, by vow, to love anyone else with an exclusive natural affection, merely for the sake of enjoying the pleasure of that love and giving human and natural consolation to another human person.

All this is true: but that does not mean that one who enters the cloister must love God in such a way that he ignores or despises other human beings. Indeed, we are commanded

[5] Cf. John 12:24-25.

to love one another as we love ourselves. But we must love others "in God." What is the meaning of the expression, "in God"? Duns Scotus tells us, very neatly.

He points out, in common with St. Thomas, that the theological virtue of Charity has really only *one* object: God. Our neighbor is not a second object, but merely an accidental object, merged, so far as we are concerned, with the first, because the same movement of the will by which we love God, catches up our neighbor, and carries him toward God with the same impetus with which we give ourselves to Him.

"By the same act," says Duns Scotus, "I desire (*volo*) God, and I will that you should desire (*velle*) Him . . . and thus, my neighbor is not assigned as a second object of my love, but as a merely accidental object . . . and I love him only in order *that he may love with me*. And thus, I love him, as it were, *accidentally, not for his own sake, but for the sake of the object which I desire to be loved by him.*"[6] And the Subtle Doctor adds: *Haec virtus habet pro objecto quietativo tantum Deum; tamen pro objecto proximo in actu reflexo, potest habere aliquid creatum.* — "This virtue has, *as the object in which it ultimately rests*, God alone; its proximate object, *by a reflex act*, may be something created."[7] The importance of that qualification, "by a reflex act" can hardly be overstressed. God always comes first, where charity is concerned.

This love of the neighbor in God is something that plays an important part in Cistercian mysticism, as will be easily recognized by anyone familiar with St. Bernard's Degrees of

---

[6] Eodem volo Deum et volo te velle Deum; et in hoc diligo te ex charitate, . . . et secundum hoc non assignatur proximus quasi secundum objectum charitatis, sed quasi omnino accidentale objectum . . . et ad hoc eum diligo ut condiligat. Et in hoc quasi accidentaliter eum diligo, non propter eum, sed propter objectum quod volo ab eo diligi (*Opus Oxoniense,* iii, d. 29).

[7] *Ibid.,* n. 5.

Humility,[8] and St. Aelred's tract on Spiritual Friendship.[9] This, in turn, is the obvious consequence of the powerful influence of the First Epistle of St. John upon Cistercian spirituality.[10]

Now St. Aelred points out a distinction between *charity,* which embraces all men, whether friends or enemies, and *spiritual friendship,* by which we are united, in God, with those who love God, by a closer bond than we ever could be united with those who hate peace and who desire only to trouble and injure us. It is quite evident that there are different classes of people that must be loved by us in this world: those whose life and thoughts and desires and aspirations are in opposition to our own, and those who harmonize with us, and seek the same end, traveling the same road. With the former we must indeed entertain a union of charity: but friendship, in the sense of free and spontaneous sharing of joys and sorrows is impossible with them. Until the barrier of opposition is broken down, this interchange cannot take place: either the conflict must cease or true friendship cannot exist. In religion, spiritual friendship is at least theoretically possible among all the members of one community, over and above the charity that must unite them as a matter of obligation. As a matter of fact, in fervent communities, the vast majority of the members are, indeed, united by true spiritual friendship, the only ones excluded being those who separate themselves and place themselves in opposition to the rest by some stubborn and incorrigible rebellion against the community, some refusal to share the joys and sorrows of the others.

One way in which a religious can cut himself off from the common union of spiritual friendship with his brethren is to

[8] Cf. Second Degree, esp. Chaps. v and vii.
[9] Migne, P.L., 195. English translation, *Christian Friendship,* by Hugh Talbot.
[10] Gilson, *Mystical Theology of St. Bernard,* p. 22.

single out one or two and enter into a *particular* friendship with them. Since such a friendship in its technical sense, is, ultimately, vicious in its source (although the offender himself may not be aware of this), it constitutes a barrier between the selfish "clique" and the virtuous majority.

Theorizing upon this point may be rather confusing, it is too abstract to be clearly grasped. But as a matter of practical fact, anyone with any experience of community life and of the consolations of the perfect charity which is spiritual friendship, will easily be able to tell the difference between it and particular friendships. Particular friendships have their roots not only in nature, but sometimes in the deepest recesses of elemental instinct and in the darkness of concupiscence. They breed envies, jealousies, unrest; they disturb the imagination and the emotions; they make prayer almost impossible. They rob the soul of peace. In fact, they are a disease which can easily blight the supernatural charm of community life.

Spiritual friendship, on the contrary, not only does not injure the supernatural life, but can be an aid to it, as St. Aelred points out. This is best explained by a concrete example. Spiritual friendship exists between those religious who, without ever being preoccupied with one another in any special way, find a constant source of joy and consolation in one another's virtues and good qualities. It can exist independently of differences in natural character and temperament — and, indeed, the test of spiritual friendship is its capacity to overlook little accidents of character that would otherwise prove repugnant to nature. Between spiritual friends there really exists the highest and purest form of love that is known on this earth: it is completely disinterested. There is no self-seeking, no desire of any personal satisfaction or consolation; in fact, not the least thought of one's own interests. This means that such love must necessarily be a source of perfect peace and tranquillity of heart, and, in fact, there is not to be found in it the slightest shadow of an inordinate passion. All is order and harmony and quietude. In our friend we seem to see the reflection of the holiness and goodness of Christ, and our thoughts and affections are raised straight to God.

Far from dwelling on the merely natural and human qualities of our friend, we lose sight of them and him together in God, who alone is the object of our love: and our friend is simply the window through which we see into the Blessed Trinity. That is to say, his virtues are such powerful evidence of his great love for God, and of God's love for him, that our own hearts are inspired, transported, and elevated to God by an increase of love and joy. The first Cistercians realized that this was one of the essential elements of the cenobitic life, and that, without this, the perfection of contemplation for a cenobite is almost impossible. Fraternal union is given us as one of our principal means for arriving at mystical union with God: for, we repeat, spiritual friendship is something that should, at least ideally, exist among *all* the members of our religious communities.

St. Aelred writes: "Therefore it need not appear strange or unnatural that we should ascend from Christ, who inspires in us the love with which we love our friend, to Christ, who offers Himself to us as a Friend to be loved. . . . And so, when friend is united to friend in the Spirit of Christ, and becomes one heart and one mind with him, he thus ascends by the degrees of love to the friendship of Christ, and becomes one spirit with Christ."[11]

We have dwelt at some length upon this topic, which is sometimes forgotten in the teaching of ascetical and mys-

[11] Non igitur videtur nimirum gravis vel innaturalis ascensus de Christo amorem inspirante, quo amicum diligimus, ad Christum, semetipsum nobis amicum praebentem quem diligamus. Itaque amicus in Spiritu Christi adhaerens amico, efficitur cum eo cor unum et anima una, et sic per amoris gradus ad Christi conscendens amicitiam, unus cum eo spiritus efficitur (St. Aelred, De Spirituali Amicitia, ii, Migne, P. L., 195, col. 672).

tical theology, and yet which was so close to the heart
of the first Cistercians and to our Lord Himself, who gave
us a new commandment: that we should love one another
as He loved us, adding: "By this shall all men know
that you are My disciples, if you have love one for another."[12]
It would be strange, indeed, if this love by which the world
must know us as Christ's disciples should consist in nothing
more than a negative observance of the precept—if it went
no further than a heroic effort to refrain from hitting each
other over the head on the slightest provocation.

Now that the importance of spiritual friendship in the contemplative life is made clear, we may pass on to the discussion
of St. Lutgarde's circle of friends, or, if you prefer, disciples
at Aywières.

The first thing that strikes us, in the consideration of this
little "school" of mysticism, is the fact that it was not mere
natural sympathy, or a common background that brought these
holy women together.

St. Lutgarde was not, indeed, of lowly birth, but her
bourgeois background and her almost total lack of education
placed her far below Sybil de Gages on the social ladder.
Sybil de Gages came from a noble family of Hainault, and
we have seen that she was well educated: so well educated,
in fact, that Jacques de Vitry urged Lutgarde to take her as a
kind of adviser and informal directress, and we have seen how
the saint had constant recourse to Sybil's superior learning.[13]

Sybil could not only read Latin fluently but also composed
verses in that tongue. She had been educated under the care
of an aunt who was Canoness at St. Gertrude's, at Nivelles,
and she eventually became herself a Canoness in that
chapter of noble and pious women. However, Christ called

[12] John 13:34-35.
[13] . . . secundum praeceptum supradicti venerabilis Jacobi (de Vitriaco)
ejusdem Sybillae consilio, ut magis litteratae, in omnibus regebatur (*Vita*,
207 b).

her to closer union with Him in the Cloister of Aywières. Sybil became a Cistercian and soon after her profession she was appointed to nurse St. Lutgarde, who was then in the infirmary, blind and practically helpless. Sybil had to help the saint get down to the church and back again, besides assisting her at meals and in all the other ordinary needs of a sick person. The nobleman's daughter did not find this easy at first. On the contrary, it caused her great repugnance to wait on her sister, and she even began to feel impatience and dissatisfaction with her lot. But finally our Lord granted her the grace of one of those interior locutions which He bestowed freely upon her patient, and Sybil heard, within her heart, the words: *Non veni ministrari, sed ministrare* — "I did not come to be ministered unto, but to minister."[14]

Repenting and swallowing her pride, Sybil gladly gave herself, and with much love, to her task, and soon there grew up a powerful supernatural affection between the two nuns. Yet Lutgarde never saw her friend's face on this earth.

"This close friendship," says an ancient French manuscript of the life of Bl. Sybil de Gages, "arose between these two souls not merely because of the fact that they lived and conversed together for several years, but also because they were of one mind, in their burning desire of perfection in every sort of virtue and their longing to attain to the highest possible degree of divine love."[15]

[14] Matt. 20:28.
[15] P. Jonquet (*op. cit.*, p. 158 ff.), quotes from this manuscript to which he had access. It is entitled: "La Vie et les Miracles de la Bienheureuse Dame Sybille de Gages, Religieuse de l'Abbaye d'Aywières," and was written by one Dom Charles Clement, spiritual director of the nuns. The date is not given, but unless P. Jonquet considerably changed the original French in his quotations, it cannot go back much further than the fifteenth century. The manuscript was, for a long time, in the possession of the Abbey of Saint-Ghislain. After the French revolution, the nephew of the last abbot of that monastery gave the manuscript to the Marquis of Gages, then owner of the ancestral castle where Sybil was born, and the document remained in his family.

Sybil outlived the saint by only four years, but died with such a reputation for heroic virtue that she was venerated as a saint herself. Jonquet quotes Arnold de Raisse's additions to the Martyrology of Molanus, where we are told of the tradition that Bl. Sybil worked many miracles in her lifetime, and how, after her death, her tomb became a place of pilgrimage. There was also a spring sacred to her memory, where the faithful came and drank and obtained relief from many bodily ills. Her relics were solemnly translated in the seventeenth century, and are preserved and venerated today in the parish church of Gages.[16]

Mystical graces are not so pronounced in the spirituality of Bl. Sybil as in that of another member of St. Lutgarde's circle, Elizabeth de Wans. Elizabeth also belonged to a noble family, this time of Liége. She had been married, but had spent the year of her married life in a purely virginal union with her husband. After a short period he died, and Elizabeth entered a convent of Benedictines at Saint-Désir, near Nogent-sur-Seine, in France where she became abbess.

However, she was glad to put off the pectoral cross and the black habit for the white cowl of a Cistercian, and became a simple religious at Aywières. Here, as a true Cistercian and disciple of St. Lutgarde, she centered her whole life of prayer upon the crucified Redeemer and reached a high degree of mystical union. It would seem that she was favored with a constant intellectual vision of Christ on the Cross that persisted without interruption for three years. We say that it was an intellectual vision, although at first sight this might not

---

[16] Jonquet, *op. cit.*, 164, n. See also a photograph of St. Sybil's reliquary, facing page 224. He calls her, throughout, "St." Sybil. This is the title on the reliquary.

It may be added that Bl. Sybil's prayers are no less powerful today than they were in the Middle Ages. When the manuscript of the present volume had been lost, the author prayed to Bl. Sybil de Gages and it was recovered within twelve hours.

be altogether evident from the original source of the story
(Rayssius, in his *Hagiologium Sanctorum Brabantiae*).[17]

Here we read: *Hanc pedetentim per tres circiter annos
Christi ad Crucem affixi statua undique sequebatur.* — "For
about three years an image of Christ on the cross followed her
everywhere she went." It might seem audacious to get an intellectual vision out of *that* — or perhaps even to get a vision
at all. However, there is a general agreement among authors
that this is to be taken as a vision, and not simply as a material
crucifix. Once that is acknowledged, we are bound, by the
authority of St. Teresa, to conclude that it was an intellectual
vision, since she assures us that imaginary visions pass very
quickly, and that only intellectual visions can extend over
long periods of time, lasting, as she says, "for several days and
even sometimes for more than a year."[18]

We are also told that whenever, during this period, Elizabeth was assailed by any kind of temptation, Christ would
detach His hand from the cross and place it on her heart, and
the temptation would go away.

Besides this she had many visions of angels and saints, and
one in which she saw all the elect gathered together in heaven,
including not a few not yet dead, and whom she had never
met. She recognized some of them afterward when she did
make their acquaintance, and was able to tell who they were
and what were their merits. Finally, one instance of the gift
of prophecy is attributed to her, although it is perhaps not
based on the most solid supernatural grounds. She saw a young
lady who was the object of much solicitude on the part of
her parents. They wanted to marry her off, and were spending
a lot of money on clothes and entertainments, to bring this
about. Elizabeth "prophesied" that this was all a waste of

[17] Quoted in the Bollandists, *vol. cit.*, 188 a., in the commentary pre-
ceding the *Vita Lutgardis*.
[18] *Interior Castle*, VI Mansions, viii, 3.

time, that she would never get herself a husband. Such prophecies do not always demand a supernatural illumination.

The new *Cistercian Menology* does not accord Elizabeth de Wans the title of Blessed, although the Bollandists do.[19] Her memory is kept in the *Cistercian Menology* on July 1, and the approximate date of her death is 1250.

The story of two other members of St. Lutgarde's circle has come down to us. The first is Yolanda, the ex-Benedictine of whom we have already spoken, and the other is Bertha of Marbais, a rich noblewoman of Namur, who was married and then left the world for the cloister after the sudden death of her husband. Her sanctity, so far as we know, was characterized by active works of charity rather than by graces of prayer. In 1227 she was sent away from Aywières to make a new foundation, under a typically poetic Cistercian name: "Our Lady's Cradle" (*Reclinatorium Beatae Virginis*). It was at Marquette, near Lille, and there she labored for twenty years as abbess, raising her community to a high degree of fervor and sanctity. Both she and Yolanda were regarded as saints.[20]

If St. Lutgarde exercised a great influence over the members of her own community, it also extended far beyond the enclosure wall of Aywières. We have seen how men and women of all ages and classes, from beggars to princes and bishops, profited by contact with her pure soul. But, after her own sisters, no group drew so much benefit and inspiration from her words and example as the members of the newly formed Order of Preachers.

It is a point of considerable historical interest that the destinies of the Friars Preachers were, at the beginning, closely

---

[19] *Loc. cit.*

[20] Bertha of Marbais is commemorated in the *Menology* on July 18. There is a tenuous probability that she was venerated with an immemorial cult. Rayssius gives Yolanda the title of Blessed, but his authority has not much weight.

interwoven with those of Citeaux. At the opening of the thirteenth century, Innocent III had ordered two Cistercian monks to leave the cloister of Fontfroide Abbey, in the hills northwest of Narbonne, and go to Toulouse as his legates, with full powers against the Albigensians. These two monks were Peter of Castelnau and a certain Ralph. As legates, they entered upon a mission that was primarily juridical and diplomatic, but soon it became evident that the corrupt rulers of Languedoc were not to be trusted, and that legal agreements with them were practically useless. The Pope conceived the plan of forming a small army of preachers, drawn from Cistercian monasteries, to travel through Languedoc fighting heresy with the sword of the spirit, which is the word of God. In fact, some monks and abbots were sent to join Peter and Ralph, under the leadership of Abbot Arnold of Citeaux. In the meantime, however, two Spaniards, Diego Bishop of Osma and a young Canon of his Cathedral Chapter, Dominic Guzman, joined forces with the Cistercian apostles at Montpellier. It was not long before it became clear that God did not want the Cistercians to forsake their cloisters, and that a new Order would soon be raised up, designed to combat error and heresy especially by its apostolic life of prayer and sacred study and preaching.

The fiery young Dominic, with his ardent love of poverty, his great humility and apostolic patience and charity was the instrument chosen by the Holy Ghost for this work, and no one saw this more clearly than the Cistercian, Foulques, who had been summoned from the Abbatial chair of Toronet to become Bishop of Toulouse, the storm center of the heresy. He gave Dominic and the companions that soon joined him every possible encouragement and advice. The first foundation made by St. Dominic and Foulques was a house of nuns at

Prouille which, in the opinion of Mandonnet,[21] was originally planned to follow the Rule of Citeaux.

What was more important, in 1213 Foulques called St. Dominic and his companions to Toulouse, and gave them a house which was to be the cradle of the Order of Friars Preachers, while, in 1215, he took Dominic to Rome to the Fourth Lateran Council, and secured the papal approbation of the new Order from Honorius III. He then presented St. Dominic with the Church of St. Roman at Toulouse, and afterward, in 1220, arranged for one sixth of the tax revenues of his diocese to be devoted to the support of the Friars.

At the same time, the new Order received much fructifying grace through the blood of the martyred Cistercian, Bl. Peter of Castelnau, in 1208.

There can be no question that St. Lutgarde, in her cloister of Aywières, with her seven-year fast against the Albigensians, which was going on just at the time when the foundations of the new Order were being laid, had also a special part to play in all this. St. Dominic's successor as General of the Friars Preachers, Bl. Jordan of Saxony, had no doubt whatever of this fact. He used to call St. Lutgarde the "Mother and nurse of the Friars Preachers."[22]

This too was deep and fruitful spiritual friendship. Bl. Jordan of Saxony had the greatest admiration for the sanctity of St. Lutgarde, and trusted her judgment completely. More than that, he placed a special confidence in her prayers and intercession for himself and his Order, and that is the sense of the title he gave her as their "Mother and nurse." From the first moment of the foundation of Citeaux, secular rulers and princes of the Church sought, with a special eagerness, to avail themselves of a share in the vast treasure of merits

---

[21] *St. Dominic and his Work*, p. 373, n.

[22] Eam totius Ordinis Praedicatorum matrem constituit et nutricem . . . (*Vita*, 205 b).

earned for the Church by the prayers of the White Monks, and here we have a case of the Master General of an entire Order placing the destinies of his Friars in the hands of one poor blind Cistercian nun. This is an indication of the importance of prayer in the life of the Church; active works, without the divine graces which only prayer and penance can obtain, are doomed to sterility and failure. This has always been the mind of the Church down to our own day.[23]

Thomas of Cantimpré, himself a fervent Dominican, tells us in some detail just what St. Lutgarde did in order to fulfill her promises to pray for the Friars Preachers. It is rather interesting to notice how she followed the trend taken by all the special prayers that used to be prescribed by the General Chapters in those days for particular intentions like peace, or salvation from barbarian invaders. She had promised Bl. Jordan that she would daily recite the Psalm "Deus misereatur nostri et benedicat nobis" and add the collect of the Holy Ghost[24] for the intentions of the Dominicans. After his death, the Master General of that Order appeared to her and made her renew her promise. She kept up the same prayers until she herself died.

We say that St. Lutgarde had a vision of Bl. Jordan. This was another and not the least important of her visions of souls, to which we have already devoted several pages.

It was about eleven years before Lutgarde passed to her reward. She had just become blind. Bl. Jordan, who had long desired to go on a pilgrimage to the Holy Land, had at last been able to fulfill his wishes as regular visitor to the Friars in the Near East. He had seen Jerusalem and Bethlehem, and was returning to Europe when, says Thomas, by the secret judgments of God, his ship, bearing a great

---

[23] Pius XI, Const. "Umbratilem."

[24] Collecta de Spiritu Sancto (*Vita*, 205 a), evidently refers to the prayer for Pentecost and Votive Masses of the Holy Ghost: "Deus Qui corda fidelium . . ."

multitude of men, and two other Friars, sank in the sea
and they were all drowned. He then proceeds to tell the
story of the miraculous recovery of their bodies, when for
five hours a pillar of fire in the night towered up to heaven
above the place where the sunken vessel lay. It must have
been near shore for, says Thomas, it was seen by many persons, Catholics, Greek schismatics, and pagans; and when the
body was cast up on the shore, the pillar of fire played over
it again, and also pointed out, in another place, the body of
his companion, Friar Gerard. Then, when the searching party
came near, and the bodies were about to be found, the pillar
of fire was drawn up into a cloud and vanished. Thomas
quotes a poetic record of this happening in iambic trimeters,
and cites the testimony of some Dominicans who said they
had seen it with their own eyes.[25]

All this was in December, 1135. On Christmas eve St.
Lutgarde spent the hours from Prime to Sext in prayer, and
all the while her soul was overwhelmed with darkness and
sorrow, so that she finally cried out: "Lord, what is this that
I feel? What is the matter?" And she added, "Indeed, if I had
any friends who would pray for me, in heaven or on earth,
I would not have such a hard heart today!"

As she was pronouncing these words through her tears,
she suddenly beheld in vision a spirit full of glory, blazing
with light. She could not tell who it might be, for the excess
of light, and she asked:

"Sir, who are you?"

"I am Friar Jordan," replied the soul, "once called Master of
the Order of Friars Preachers. I have passed out of this world
and into glory, and I am exalted to a place among the choirs
of the Apostles and Prophets. And lo, now I am sent to thee,
to bring thee consolation in this most joyous feast." And then

[25] *Vita*, 204 e.

he earnestly added his injunction that she should continue
her prayers for his Order.

We have already seen something of her relations with other
individual Dominicans, in speaking of her friendship with
Jacques de Vitry and with her biographer Thomas of
Cantimpré. Indeed, the latter's *Vita Lutgardis* tells us of the
spiritual benefits which they both derived from their friendship in Christ. This is an example of the way in which Christ
intended and planned the sanctification of His whole Church,
by the mutual interaction of souls obedient to the Holy Spirit.
He wills to save us all, through the free actions of our own
wills, in correspondence to the motions and direction of the
Spirit of Love, and His reason for doing so is that we may,
by saving others, participate more fully in the fruits of divine
Love, becoming ever more and more closely united with Him
through this mutual co-operation with one another in prayer
and good works.

So, too, by her prayers and charity St. Lutgarde participated
in the merits of all the good works of the Dominicans and
other apostolic workers for whom she prayed, and through her
the graces and merits of Cistercian prayer and penance were
transmitted to them.

Before closing this chapter and passing on to a consideration of St. Lutgarde's last years and death, we may, in a sense,
sum up her life by a brief comparison of her spirituality with
that of several other Cistercian mystics. This will serve to
establish her place in Cistercian history, as well as to introduce one or two names which the reader would otherwise
never hear.

There is one thing which the great saints have in common: they are all simple. It is a paradox, but it is true nevertheless: the more divine their lives are, the more human they
become. The more their love is supernaturalized, the more
natural do they appear to us. We are here using the word

"natural" to signify the ease and simplicity, the harmonious
co-ordination of nature and grace, by which we recognize
that grace has attained such mastery over the soul as to become its second nature. When we call the great saints "natural" and "human" we are no longer referring to the weakness
and limitations of fallen nature, but to the transcendent
simplicity of nature emancipated by grace: the easy freedom
of a true child of God, who wears the divine sonship as a
garment to which he is accustomed, and not as something
new and awkward and uncomfortable, making every act seem
false and strained.

One gets the impression that St. Lutgarde, for all her
sublime and magnificent mystical love for Christ, was by
no means an ethereal, wraithlike figure, barely walking on the
earth, always pale, and half absorbed in dreams. On the contrary, she strikes us as very real and very matter of fact and
very Flemish. We see her spitting at the devils that bothered
her in her prayers. We see her leaning against the wall, bleeding and in ecstasy, and yet she is not afraid to make a sign
to her sisters, and to offer them human consolation in their
troubles, without artifice or embarrassment.

Her humility was of the kind that does not even remember
to comment upon itself, and to call attention to its own short-
comings. She had passed far beyond that, and was occupied
totally with God, utterly forgetful of herself. Nevertheless,
she never entered into such a state that she forgot others in
her prayers, or refused to pray for them. On the contrary, she
used to besiege heaven in their behalf with the most ardent
and simple passion and desire. But the thing that strikes us
most about her is the fact that her eyes were always on the
crucified Christ, and on His Cross, not in a strained and
wearying absorption that is largely reflexive and is always
reaching out for new "experiences" and fresh consolations,
but in a direct and intense and utterly simple love for the

Person of Jesus, for the Sacred Heart who so loved her. She
loved Him for His sake more than for her own. Her soul was
united with Him who is pure love, and she was supremely
content with that union, with that love, seeking nothing else
for there is nothing better or more perfect that could possibly be sought than to love God as He loves Himself, with
His own infinite love. *Verus amor seipso contentus est. Habet
praemium, sed id quod amatur.* St. Bernard's words are hard
to translate: let us leave them in Latin, and say that their
meaning is simply that true love is content with itself and only
has a reward in the sense that it is its own reward.[26]

Since we have mentioned St. Bernard, we may begin by
comparing St. Lutgarde with the great Cistercian mystics of
the twelfth century. The first thing that must be said, then,
is that while St. Lutgarde puts into practice the teachings of
the great speculative mystics of the previous century, she
does not quite attain to the heights and to the vast sweep of
the mysticism of St. Bernard, or even of St. Aelred, Bl. Guerric,
or William of St. Thierry. But, of course, it is hard to compare
them. On the one hand, we have the writings of great doctors, in which profound learning in Scripture and dogma is
mingled with the unction of wisdom and mystical experience;
and on the other, we have the visions of St. Lutgarde. But
as for the real depths of the mystical life and experiences of
St. Bernard and St. Aelred, we know very little, at least directly. Their writings allow us to guess, and sometimes we
obtain a direct hint: and always we find them teaching that
visions and lofty mystical consolations are relatively unim-
portant, mere accidents of the true life of union. As for the
numerous visions which were related as indications of
the heights of St. Bernard's mystical life, they simply reflect

[26] *De Diligendo Deo,* vii, 17. Gilson, *Mystical Theology of St. Bernard,*
p. 141 ff., clearly distinguishes between the concept of "pure love" in
Cistercian mystical theology and that taught by the quietists.

the inability of the average man to grasp just how high the saint had actually risen. Many of them are legendary, and where there may be a foundation of truth, it is hard to discover just how much truth is really there. The authentic biographers of the saint place little stress on his visions,[27] and Vacandard does not accept the legend of the so-called "lactation" by the Mother of God as worthy of equal respect with the *Sermons on the Canticle of Canticles* as evidence of the saint's mysticism.[28]

St. Lutgarde has all of St. Bernard's love for the humanity of our Blessed Saviour, but her mysticism does not ascend, like his, into the very bosom of the Trinity. Nevertheless, if we consider her from another angle, we see that she represents a definite development over St. Bernard in the direction of the modern devotion to the Sacred Heart which, though not explicit in the writings of the saint of Clairvaux, begins to take definite shape in the spirituality of St. Lutgarde.

This naturally leads us to the consideration of the great Cistercian mystic of the Sacred Heart who flourished in Germany at the end of St. Lutgarde's century. We mean St. Gertrude of Helfta.[29] Inseparable from her is her mistress in the mystical life, St. Mechtilde of Hackeborn. In the writings of these two great saints we first find the devotion to the Sacred Heart of Jesus fully developed. They have all St. Lutgarde's ardor and tenderness, and much of her funda-

---

[27] By these we mean Bl. William of St. Thierry, Ernald of Bonnevaux, and Geoffrey of Auxerre, the compilers of the *Vita Prima*.

[28] Vacandard, *Vie de Saint Bernard*, Vol. ii, p. 78.

[29] Helfta was not actually incorporated into the Cistercian Order, since at the time of its foundation the General Chapter had forbidden the acceptance of any new convents into the Order. However, the nuns kept the Cistercian Rule, but they had Benedictines for their spiritual directors since the Chapter had also forbidden Cistercian priests to undertake the direction of non-Cistercians — in fact, this went back to the first statutes of the Order. This accounts for the long-standing confusion as to whether St. Gertrude was a Cistercian or a Benedictine. See *Compendium of the History of the Cistercian Order*, p. 97.

mental simplicity. But St. Lutgarde never wrote a line. On
the contrary, St. Gertrude and St. Mechtilde were not only
writers, they were, in a sense, intellectuals. Their mystical
writings represent the full flowering of that allegorical spirituality characteristic of the High Middle Ages. Their ideas
and images are complex, vivid, and, at times, lavish, gorgeous,
dazzling. Both of these saints did more than merely
follow the liturgy: they exploited it to the full. There was not
a Mass, not an Office in the whole liturgical year, whose
treasures had not been ransacked by these two immensely
gifted saints.

St. Lutgarde had to ask Sybil de Gages to explain the
simplest Latin phrase to her: St. Gertrude and St. Mechtilde
were, without exaggeration, theologians, although they had
never had any formal training in this science.

The chief reason why their writings[30] are so valuable to
religious is that they contain a fully developed ascetical and
mystical doctrine, with its roots deep in the liturgy, and expressed in terms easy for the simplest minds to understand.
They provide ideal books of meditation for those who need
them. It is interesting to notice the close relation of St. Gertrude's teachings on confidence, humility, and love to the Little
Way of St. Thérèse of Lisieux. As a matter of fact, the Cistercians of Helfta were the direct spiritual ancestors of the
Little Flower. The line of descent is easily traced through the
French School of the seventeenth century and St. Margaret
Mary Alacoque.

Two of the three Cistercian "Idas," contemporaries of Lutgarde in thirteenth-century Flanders, were, like her, almost

---

[30] *Le Héraut de l'Amour Divin, Révélations de Sainte Gertrude,* Paris,
1877; *Le Livre de Grace Spéciale, Révélations de Sainte Mechtilde* —
French versions of the Latin edition of the Benedictines of Solesmes. The
revelations of St. Mechtilde were taken down by the younger saint, and
come to us from her pen. Several separate works of St. Gertrude are
available in English.

totally absorbed in the same consuming love of the divine humanity, with this difference that they were attracted more explicitly and exclusively to Christ in the Blessed Sacrament. Bl. Ida of Louvain was perhaps the most emphatically Eucharistic of the Cistercian saints.[31] Bl. Ida of Léau used to spend hours in simple absorption before the divine Prisoner in the tabernacle. This was her prayer and her mysticism, and it led her to a profoundly intimate union with Jesus. Both these saints, also, had visions of Christ in the form of a Child, usually in connection with the Mass or the Blessed Sacrament. Ida of Louvain was sometimes rather extreme in her excesses of mystical love. Once, she was hardly able to restrain herself from breaking into the tabernacle to see her Beloved. There was none of this in St. Lutgarde. However, charming as was the great and romantic saint of Aywières, there is scarcely any Cistercian mystic that can approach the delightful candor and simplicity of Bl. Ida of Léau, who is certainly one of our loveliest and most attractive saints. It is a great pity that she is not better known — her life, by a contemporary monk, lies hidden in the pages of the Bollandists.[32] Bl. Ida of Léau (Leeuwen) was a nun of Ramège (La Ramée), where she reached a high degree of prayer and mystical union, but was also an accomplished copyist of manuscripts in the nuns' *scriptorium*. Once the Blessed Virgin appeared to her in choir, and placed the Child Jesus in her arms just as she was about to sing a responsory. The usages demand that the arms be "in ceremony," that is, hanging at one's sides, when singing a responsory. Bl. Ida did not know what to do, but she exclaimed: "Take care of Yourself, Lord, it is my turn to

[31] Bl. Ida Louvain, died about 1300 in the convent of Roosendael, was famous for her visions. She had been stigmatized, also. She is commemorated in the *Cistercian Menology*, April 13, and her memory is venerated with a feast in certain dioceses of Belgium, where she is one of the national patrons. Her biography may be found in *Acta Sanctorum*, April, ii, 156.
[32] *Acta Sanctorum*, October, xiii, 100. *Cistercian Menology*, Oct., 29.

sing," and the Child Jesus threw His arms around her neck
and clung to her while she sang her responsory — and sang it,
we are told, better that she ever sang anything before or
afterward.

Of the three Idas, perhaps the one who most resembles
St. Lutgarde is Bl. Ida of Nivelles, another nun of Ramège.
She had much the same simple and ardent temperament as
St. Lutgarde, and came close to her in her intensely unselfish
zeal in praying for souls, especially sinners, and the poor
sufferers in purgatory. Even more than Lutgarde, she had to
contend with the enmity of devils but treated them with no
less contempt than the dauntless saint of Aywières. When
the fiends appeared to her in the form of various animals she
would send them packing with a good kick.[33]

Finally, Bl. Beatrice of Nazareth resembles St. Gertrude
more than St. Lutgarde. In fact, her prayer tends toward systematic allegory, without losing its fundamental simplicity and
its affective character. She was also a mystic, and her
mysticism was profoundly liturgical. There is in her much
more of the intellectual and of the conscious artist than
there is in St. Lutgarde.[34]

The two royal saints of Portugal, SS. Teresa and Sancha,[35]
were, it is true, mystics: but they are above all remarkable as
foundresses of convents and as austere penitents.

There were many other Cistercian mystics in the monas-

[33] *Cistercian Menology*, December 11. Her original life is edited by
Henriquez in his *Quinque Prudentes Virgines*, p. 199.
[34] In fact, she is one of the few Cistercians who have left us an autobiography. She was commemorated on July 28 in the old *Menology* and
will probably be commemorated on the real date of her death, August 29,
in the new edition.
[35] See *Acta Sanctorum*, June, IV, 385; *Menology*, June 17 and March
13. They were both princesses of the royal house of Portugal. St. Teresa
founded Lorvao, and St. Sancha built a monastery at Celles. A third
sister, Bl. Mafalda, was a Cistercian nun at Arouca.

teries of our monks during St. Lutgarde's century. We need only mention Villers, so close to Aywières, in the same province of Brabant, and once so famous for the holiness of its members that it was called "Villers-la-sainte." Bl. Arnulph, a lay brother of that famous community, has little of St. Lutgarde's balance and intensity of single-minded love. He was rather an enthusiast, and was so carried away by his passion for penance that he practiced weird and extraordinary flagellations and excelled in inventing new methods of torturing his flesh. He had many visions, but his mysticism tended to be noisy and disturbing to others, ending in outbursts of spiritual intoxication that disrupted the good order of community exercises. Nevertheless, for all his extravagance, this brother has some of the charm and originality of the saints of the "Fioretti."[36]

Bl. Simon of Aulne has been mentioned several times in the course of this book. He was even more famous than St. Lutgarde as a seer, and possessed extraordinary gifts of prophecy and insight into souls; but he did not have so much of her intimate love for and union with Christ crucified. It is interesting, too, to remark that all those who had less of this strong and personal and all-embracing love of Christ were more given to extreme bodily mortifications and voluntary penances and sufferings. They were, in fact, often simply athletes of penance. St. Lutgarde's fasts were extraordinary, but they merge into her mystical union with the sufferings of Christ, and are, by their plainly supernatural character, elevated above the sphere of merely voluntary mortifications. For the most part, as we have seen, her sufferings were not self-imposed, but chosen and given to her by God in the form of shattering illnesses and trials, ending in her blindness.

[36] *Acta Sanctorum*, June, vii, 556; *Menology*, June 30.

In this respect, the Cistercian saint that approaches St. Lutgarde the most closely is Bl. Alice, or Aleyde[37] of La Cambre. For many years, this holy nun was imprisoned in a little cell, apart from the community, infected with the living death of leprosy. Yet, many who came to her with this and with other diseases were cured. However, her vocation was not that of a miracle worker, so much as of a "victim soul" for the sins of the world. She had an exceptionally strong realization of the fact that the salvation of many individual souls depended upon her acceptance of these sufferings from the hand of God. As her disease progressed she lost the sight of first one eye, then the other, offering them up for William, King of the Romans, and St. Louis of France, who was then fighting in Palestine. Added to all her other trials were the intense purgative fires of infused love and the dark night of the soul. She died in 1249.

But all that has been said so far must not obscure the fact that these thirteenth-century Cistercian mystics with whom we have mostly been dealing do not represent the pure Cistercian spirituality that characterized the first century of the Order's history. In St. Lutgarde we find practically nothing of that beautiful and simple zeal which was the very foundation stone of the Order—the zeal for the Rule of St. Benedict in its purity, the zeal for labor in the fields, silence, solitude, community life, monastic simplicity, and that concern with doing ordinary things quietly and perfectly for the glory of God, which is the beauty of pure Benedictine life. Of course, St. Lutgarde was Cistercian and Benedictine in her spirituality, in her love of the Divine Office, in her love of Christ above all else; but she lacks this Benedictine *plainness,* and this Cistercian technique of humility which consists in a kind of protective coloring, by which the monk

---

[37] *Acta Sanctorum,* June, ii, 471. Her feast is kept in the Cistercian Order of the Strict Observance on June 12, as a feast of three lessons.

simply disappears into the background of the common, every-day life, like those birds and animals whose plumage and fur make them almost indistinguishable from their surroundings.

This does not and cannot imply a criticism of St. Lutgarde herself. It was not her fault that Christ singled her out, by means of extraordinary graces and sufferings, from the rest of her sisters and from the rest of the world. After all, in the first great days of the Order He did the same thing with St. Bernard of Clairvaux, making him the apostle of Europe and the adviser of popes and kings. Besides, we must not wonder that she did not explicitly concern herself with the purity of the Rule in the same way as did the Fathers of the Order who had left Molesme for the sole purpose of re-establishing the Rule in its literal integrity. We only mention the contrast, and point out that, after all, the essence of Cistercianism is not so much in the extraordinary sufferings of St. Lutgarde as in the ordinary penances of a life of labor and solitude and silence and obedience. But in any case: there must always be one thing above all: burning love for Jesus.

CHAPTER EIGHT

LAST YEARS AND DEATH
OF ST. LUTGARDE

WE HAVE considered a few cases of prophetic insight and of revelation in the life of St. Lutgarde. One or two others might also have been mentioned, for example her prophecy of the return of an apostate Friar Minor to his Order,[1] and her vision identifying the relics of an unknown saint. The second incident concerned the discovery of some relics at the monastery of Jouarre, near Meaux, in France. They were in an alabaster tomb in a chapel crypt, and the priest who had discovered them, having failed by ordinary means to find out whose relics they were, asked St. Lutgarde to pray for a revelation concerning them.

In due course, the forgotten saint appeared to Lutgarde and declared that she was St. Osmanna, a virgin and daughter of the King of Ireland, who had come to France and taken up her dwelling in Brittany, where she had led a very holy life.[2]

---

[1] *Vita,* 202 d. The good Dominican, Thomas of Cantimpré, hastens to add that one should not be astonished that a man should apostatize even from so excellent an Order as that of the Franciscans, when there was a traitor even in that most perfect religious community: Christ's twelve Apostles.

[2] *Vita,* 202 c. Ego vocor Osanna (sic) virgo, filia quondam Regis Scotiae et per miraculum Domini ad partes Galliae adducta, sancte vixi. . . . *Scotia* refers to Ireland as well as Scotland, cf. the *Martyrology* (Cistercian) for March 17: "In *Scotia,* Sancti Patritii. . . ." The Bollandists refer us to Henry Fitzsimmon, *Catalogus Sanctorum Hiberniae,* where St. Osmanna is referred to as being venerated variously on Sept. 10 and Nov. 22 (204,

Lutgarde asked the Irish saint to confirm this by appearing also to the priest from Jouarre, which she did, with great promptness and generosity, not only once but three times in succession.

Most of St. Lutgarde's prophecies concerned her own death. The vision of Bl. Jordan of Saxony, which we have mentioned, was not intended merely to inform her of the shipwreck and loss of the General of the Friar's Preachers, but also to let her know that her own reward was soon to come.[3]

Five years before her death, that is, in 1241, St. Lutgarde received the revelation that she would enter heaven on the third Sunday after Pentecost, when the Gospel of the Great Marriage Feast would be sung.[4]

Meanwhile, she had been totally blind for the past six years, that is since 1235. Besides that, since 1239, she had been carrying on her third and last seven-year fast on bread and a few vegetables, to save the Church from the power-politics of Emperor Frederick II.

The strictness of her fast may be judged from the fact that she did not even mitigate it on Easter Sunday but fasted relentlessly every day for the whole seven years. It must be remembered that the Cistercian Order at that time kept the black fast for most of the year, the single meal of the day being taken at three o'clock in the afternoon during the winter season, and in the evening, after Vespers, in Lent. Also, the term "bread and vegetables" is apt to be a little vague, as this is all that any Cistercian is likely to get, even today. For St. Lutgarde, it evidently signified a meal consisting of bread and an onion or a little lettuce or a raw carrot, so that to all intents and purposes she was cutting her food down

---

n. b.) Her relics were translated to St. Denis, from Brittany. But evidently some also went to Jouarre.

[3] Tu autem jam secura esto de praemio: quia in proximo est ut a Domino coroneris (*Vita*, 205 a).

[4] Luke 14:16. *Vita*, 205 e.

to the minimum. She was ill in the infirmary all this time, and would, ordinarily, have been entitled to every mitigation, and even to the use of flesh meat.

Although she did not live to see the effect of her fast, she was able to prophesy, in all confidence, that Frederick II would be laid low and the Church saved from his depredations, as we have seen. When Thomas of Cantimpré was setting down the record of her life, this prophecy was not yet fulfilled. But he said: "Not one of the things she prophesied has been seen to fail, which is a clear proof that what she said was inspired by the Holy Ghost."[5]

In the years that followed St. Lutgarde's death, Frederick II, marching against Pope Innocent IV who had excommunicated him (1245, Council of Lyons), was defeated with his army that included many thousands of Saracens. After that, his power crumbled. The Emperor turned against his own henchmen, poisoning one, starving another to death, while a third only escaped being blinded and turned over to his worst enemies by beating out his own brains against the stone pillar to which he was chained. Finally, in 1250, the Emperor himself died suddenly, and it is thought that he was strangled by one of his natural sons.

This is the way it will always be with those who hate God and His Church. Indeed, one might say that it is not even necessary for God to take the trouble to punish them: all He has to do is to leave them to themselves. But that, precisely, is what it means to be punished by God: to be abandoned by Him, and left at the mercy of perverted human nature and of the devils of hell.

Frederick II and his Saracen allies were not the only danger threatening the Church in those days. A far more terrible and

---

[5] Neque enim unum ex omnibus quae futura praedixit per annihilationem in terra vidimus excidisse, utpote illius verba, quae in Spiritu Dei hausisse plenissime comprobatur (*Vita*, 205 c).

more universal scourge was hanging over the entire civilization of the western world.

During the years when St. Lutgarde had been living in the obscure and silent cloister of Aywières, when St. Dominic had been founding his Order, and when the Franciscans and Dominicans had been raising Christian learning and science to the highest perfection in the Schools of Paris and Oxford, and when St. Louis had mounted the throne of France, a strange and terrible storm had been raging over the deserts of Asia.

Who has not heard at least the name of the mysterious barbarian leader, Genghis Khan, that cunning and insatiable savage who, with his armies of merciless followers conquered the entire width of Asia from Persia to China, to leave his heirs an empire vaster and richer than Alexander or Napoleon ever dreamed of? They say his armies wiped out some five or six million men.

Genghis Khan had died in 1237, but his sons, no less fierce than he, had turned toward Europe, had overrun Russia, Poland, and Hungary, while the Carizmians, no less barbarous than the Mongols themselves, had retreated before their more powerful adversaries, only to descend upon the Holy Land, take Jerusalem, and profane the Holy Sepulcher.

Western Europe now seemed to be at the mercy of the new barbarian invasion. A Crusade was proclaimed by Innocent IV at the Council of Lyons, and the Christian armies marched against the Mongols in Silesia, only to go down in defeat before the wild men on little shaggy horses, fast as the winds of the Gobi desert.

It is not hard to imagine what was now in store for Europe, weakened and divided by the wars and policies of Frederick II, and by the many antipopes and by all the other conflicting interests that had kept the Christian world in such confusion for the past century.

Thomas of Cantimpré writes: "Four years before her death, the exceedingly cruel race of Tartars, pouring forth from their own lands, destroyed Greater Hungary to the East and Lesser Hungary to the West, together with the major part of Turkey and Greece, with Bulgaria and Russia, killed the most powerful Duke of Poland, and laid waste his lands, putting his people to the sword. And when they now began to invade part of Germany, namely Bohemia, there came a great fear over all Germany and over France, lest the Tartars ravage them, as they had ravaged all those other lands."[6]

At this juncture, Fra Bernard, the Dominican, St. Lutgarde's other spiritual director, of whom there is frequent mention in the *Vita*,[7] came to her in fear and confusion, terrified by the crisis, and begging her to intercede before the throne of God.

That was in 1242.[8]

To the consternation of the good friar, St. Lutgarde was not in the least disturbed by the alarming news he brought her. One would have thought that a poor helpless woman, an invalid, totally blind, might have been at least slightly perturbed at the thought of thousands of little yellow men rushing around with swords and setting fire to everything. But St. Lutgarde was completely unruffled.

"Why," she said coolly, "I have not yet even begun to pray to our Lord concerning this business. I am quite certain that now these Tartars will never come into our country."

Fra Bernard accepted this news as a prophecy, which indeed it was, and went away much relieved.

In 1243, Oktai, the son of Genghis Khan and the leader of the Mongol armies, died, and his followers, bereft of their commander, lost all their moral support and, disintegrating

---

[6] *Vita*, 205 e.
[7] He was the Pope's penitentiary.
[8] Quarto anno ante mortem ejus (*Vita*, 205 f).

into small bands, returned into Asia. Europe was saved.

All this time, however, St. Lutgarde was growing more and more impatient for the day of her release from the limitations and imperfection of this life, in order to enter into that perfect life in which there is no longer any shadow of an obstacle between ourselves and our God. We have seen how the impetuous violence of the infused desire of martyrdom in her soul had resulted in the mystical piercing of her heart, outwardly manifested by a real and physical wound. But this love was no transitory thing. It had become a more or less constant state with her, and so great were her sufferings (if we may judge from Thomas of Cantimpré, and from the light which St. Teresa also throws upon this subject) that they did constitute a martyrdom for her — and a far greater and more terrible and more purifying martyrdom than that of illness and blindness or any other natural affliction.

The soul in such a state as this, says St. Teresa,[9] is sometimes so afflicted with the thought that its death is being indefinitely delayed, that it is pierced with a supernatural anguish as sudden and as destructive as a thunderbolt, which strikes at the very depths and center of the soul and "reduces all the earthly part of our nature to powder." Under the violence of this impact, the soul loses consciousness to the extent that it no longer has the strength to move itself in any way, and yet this trance only serves to heighten the agony and make it more intense. "The understanding," writes the saint, "realizes acutely what cause there is for grief in separation from God, and His Majesty now augments this sorrow by a vivid manifestation of Himself." And she adds: "The person I speak of [meaning of course herself] learnt from this how much more acutely the spirit is capable of suffering than the body; she understood that this resembled the pains of purgatory, where the absence of the flesh does not prevent

---

[9] *Interior Castle*, VI Mansions, Chap. xi.

the torture being far worse than any we can feel in this world."[10]

With St. Lutgarde, then, the desire of heaven was something more than a pious wish. It was a mystical affliction that united her with Christ on Calvary. Some learned director of mystical souls — Thomas of Cantimpré does not tell us his name — declared that he had never seen anyone who equaled the perfection of faith with which St. Lutgarde lived beyond and outside of this world, "absent from the body and present to the Lord."[11]

Thomas himself testifies that he sometimes saw her weeping so piteously in her disappointment that she was not yet dead and able to enter into heaven, that he himself could not bear to look at her without being moved to tears.[12]

In 1244 it seemed for a time that she would have her wish. She fell gravely ill, and Fra Bernard, calling at Aywières, found that she had been given the Last Sacraments, as though she were expected to die at any moment. At this, of course, the saint was in a high state of enthusiasm and delight. But the Father decided that he saw no evidence that she was about to leave this world, and told her so.

"Oh, don't say that, dear Father," cried St. Lutgarde, "for indeed I greatly desire to see Christ, face to face."

"Truly, Mother, you will not see Him now," said the priest.

"Well," she said, lifting up her eyes to heaven, "if I am not to see Him now, at least may His will be done tomorrow. Let me get up and I will at least receive Him in Communion."[13]

[10] *Ibid.*, Stanbrook trans., p. 219.

[11] Quidam vitae spiritualis expertissimus praedicator, dixit: "Quod numquam sicut piam Lutgardem aliquem in vita cognovit, ita perfecte per fidem migrantem in intellectum et affectum" (*Vita*, 206 e). Cf. 2 Cor. 5:8.

[12] Vidi ipse in hoc aliquando lacrymas ejus tantas, quod vix eas aliquis sine lacrymis sustinere valeret (*Vita*, 206 e).

[13] *Vita*, 206 f.

St. Lutgarde was not so absorbed in her desire of heaven
that she remained indifferent to everything that went on
around her on earth. With characteristically blunt simplicity
she had observed that the nuns in the infirmary were reciting
their Office in a rather careless manner, and she told them
that their execution of this duty could be considerably im-
proved. Also she did not hesitate to warn them that if they
did not do better the convent as a whole would be given
grave cause to regret their neglect: a prophecy which Thomas
of Cantimpré considers to have been fulfilled after her death,
as we shall presently see.

Nor was the saint so engrossed with her own entrance into
bliss that she no longer prayed for anyone else. On the contrary, she interceded for one sinner in terms which, considering her circumstances, were truly heroic. A friend of hers in
the world had fallen into a sin, and had confessed it, but
after his confession he still had no peace. He was weighed
down with utter hopelessness and despaired of pardon. He
did, however, have the strength to seek the assistance of St.
Lutgarde, confiding in her as if she were his own mother,
and begging her to obtain grace for him from God.

Twice, three times she assailed the walls of heaven with
the most fervent prayers, without receiving any apparent
answer. Her sinner was just as hopeless as before, and she
herself was aware of no internal sign that her prayer had
been heard—although such graces seem to have been more
or less constantly granted her at this time.

This, however, only stimulated her courage and her desires.
In all her prayers, St. Lutgarde's faith amounted to a kind
of holy stubbornness. Apparent failure was only a challenge
to her ardent soul. So now, says Thomas, she began to wrestle
with the Lord,[14] and finally, when she saw that God persisted

[14] In oratione cum Domino mira spiritus instantia luctabatur . . .
(*Vita*, 207 e).

in withholding His mercy she cried out: "Well, then, either wipe my name out of the book of life, or forgive this man his sin."

In St. Lutgarde's state, on the very doorsill of an eternity which she desired with all the strength of her loving heart, deletion from the book of life was not merely a metaphor, a vague and outworn phrase without very much meaning. Yet she could say such a prayer! But, of course, we have to understand precisely what it implies. After all, the words sprang from a heart that was a burning furnace of confident love and there could simply be no question in her mind that God could delete her from the book of life on such terms. In other words, she was simply playing His mercy against His justice in a way that showed how well she knew that His mercy was the stronger. It was as if she had said: "You know that Your love will not allow You to wipe my name out of the book of life without cause: therefore let that same love override Your justice, and hear my prayer, since You love me." This acknowledgment that His mercy must, indeed, prove invincible was all that God was waiting for. He rewarded her by not only answering her prayer, but by praising her for her trust, and, because of that trust, promising to make her His mercy's special instrument.

"Behold, I have forgiven him, because he has had confidence in *you*," said our Lord to St. Lutgarde, "and not to him alone, but also to all those who hope in you, and who are loved by you, will I display My bounty and My love."[15]

One of St. Bernard's most characteristic themes is his insistence that God only appears not to hear our prayers in order to stir us up to pray with all the more fervor and love.[16]

---

[15] Ecce dimisi illi quia confisus est de te: et non solum illi, sed et omnibus qui spem habent in te, et diliguntur a te, benefaciam propter tè (*Vita*, 207 f).

[16] Cf., for instance, *Sermon 74 in Cantica*, 3–5.

And then, too, we ourselves should take advantage of this promise. After all, it was given not so much for St. Lutgarde's benefit as for our own. God, in His infinite desire to bring us all to the eternal delight of participating in His own love of His own Nature, which is Love Itself, has given us the saints that by our love and confidence in them we may come to Him more rapidly and more easily. God wants us all to participate in the joys and benefits of one another's salvation. In a sense, too, it gives God greater glory when we trust in His operation through a weak and fallible instrument, than when we trust in His omnipotence working in its own sphere.

But, to continue with her story, as it draws closer and closer to the end: in 1245 Christ appeared to her, this time in a most joyful and gratifying vision. His face, says Thomas, was that of one congratulating her and applauding her for her fortitude and patience. And He said to her: "Now the end of your labors is at hand. I will not have you be separated much longer from Me. Three things alone I require of you in this coming year. . . . "

So there was to be one more year! Yes, and this last year was to crown all her labors. What were these works which Christ deigned to assign to her by His own personal command?

"First," said our Lord, "I would have you render thanks to Me for all the benefits that you have received." Thanksgiving, then, was to be the principal factor in bringing her whole life of sacrifice and adoration to its culminating perfection. What a way to prepare for our death: by thanking God for all the gifts and graces He has bestowed upon us, from the creation of our souls, at conception, and their recreation at baptism, through all the vicissitudes of life. St. Lutgarde could thank her God that His special graces had not only kept her free from sin, but had enabled her to walk the paths of the most sublime and heroic sanctity. To thank

Him for all this was a task far beyond the power of her own poor prayers, and our Lord added: "In this you will require the prayers of the Blessed in heaven, to assist you."

"The second thing I ask of you," Jesus continued, "is to pour yourself out entirely, in prayers for My sinners, before the throne of My Father."

In other words, in this last year of her life, she was to intensify her zeal in performing what had been one of the principal labors of her career. But there was one thing that had occupied her even more, all her years in the convent, than the love of souls: that was her love of God, her desire of union with Him. This was the third labor Christ imposed upon her, to perfect and bring to a climax her life of love and sacrifice: an intensification of *desire*.

"The third thing I ask of you," said Jesus, "is that you should yearn to come to Me, with the most avid of desires, to the exclusion of every other thought, every other care."[17]

Reflecting upon these three points, we can easily see that they offer us a good summary of the contemplative, cloistered vocation. These are the things to which the literal observance of the Rule of St. Benedict should bring the monk: they are the interior dispositions which are the immediate and proximate end of all our external mortifications and practices of penance and our liturgical prayer.

Thanksgiving, intercession for sinners, and an all-absorbing desire for union with God — a desire that burns in the soul like a raw and bleeding wound and which embodies perfect adoration: these three give perfect and practical expression to the twofold commandment which sums up the whole law and the prophets.[18] *Diliges!* Thou shalt love! Love God with

---

[17] Tertium est quod venire ad me sine aliqua alia solicitudine hianti desiderio concupiscas (*Vita*, 207 b).

[18] Matt. 22:37–40.

thy whole heart and thy whole soul and with thy whole mind, and thy neighbor as thyself.

Christ came in Person to ask St. Lutgarde to spend the last year of her life in the all-exclusive exercise of the contemplative and Christian life in its perfection, that we might learn, from this, how He desires us to live, and how He would have us prepare for death.

Someone will ask: "What about penance?" But, of course, penance is eminently contained in the ardor of the love which Christ was here demanding of His saint — there is no more perfect way of wiping out our own sins and of atoning for the sins of the world than by love, while, conversely, only love, and a love divinely infused, could enable any soul to bear the torture of that last year of St. Lutgarde's separation from God.

To relieve the burning anguish of His spouse, dying of love for Him, Christ and His Virgin Mother appeared to St. Lutgarde in the Paschal time of 1246. Her death was now only a month or two away. They had come with joy and gladness to tell her so, and to assuage her longings. "It is not fitting, My dear," said Jesus to her, "that you should wear yourself out with sorrow and yearning any more: for even now the solace of everlasting peace is being prepared, to be your crown! We do not want to keep you waiting longer."[19]

Overwhelmed with awe and exultation, St. Lutgarde communicated this to Bl. Sybil de Gages, as she had communicated most of her other visions and revelations. *Maximo timore et exultatione,* are the words used by Thomas of Cantimpré, to describe her reaction.[20] *Timore?* With fear? How so? But this was not the fear of her divine Judge on account of sins. It was

---

[19] Non te oportet, Carissima, ab hoc praesenti tempore ulterius fatigari; jam tibi remedium perpetuae pacis disponitur ad coronam; nec te volumus amodo diutius expectare (*Vita,* 207 b).

[20] *Ibidem.*

not servile fear. It was that holy fear, that loving awe at the tremendous might and majesty of God, which causes the Seraphim to veil themselves with their wings and cry aloud to one another: "Holy, Holy, Holy, the Lord God of Hosts, all the earth is full of His glory!"[21]

Far from shaking her confidence in God, this combination of exultancy and fear was a sign that her loving confidence had brought her to the very doorsill of the Holy of Holies. She was about to enter into the Sanctuary of Heaven, and view His tremendous glory without the shadow of a veiling intermediary. To stand in the gate of death without this grand and inspired awe would seem to argue that one would have to wait some time in the antechamber, instead of entering into the throne room of the King without delay.

Paschal time drew to its close. Around the quiet, secluded convent of Aywières, the May flowers began to enamel with their blooms the green pastures, and all the valley was filled with the freshness of the spring foliage of the poplars along the water courses. The mild, peaceful, hazy mornings of Flanders' early summer tempered the heat of the sun as it climbed toward the June solstice. With the Feast of the Ascension, the liturgical Christ bade farewell to the white choir of His disciples, and rose to heaven, treading the bright air. And then, at Pentecost, the Holy Spirit showered His Church once more with fiery graces. And in that shower, there was another, special favor for the dying saint at Aywières.

A few days after Whitsunday, in the great Pentecostal octave, the glorious Virgin Mary, together with St. John the Baptist, to whom St. Lutgarde had such a fervent devotion, appeared to her with the glad news: "Your consummation is at hand. Your crown of justice is waiting for you. We

[21] Isa. 6:2–3.

would not have you remain longer on earth: all the citizens
of heaven are on the watch for your coming."[22] But Thomas
adds that repeatedly, during that year, first one saint, then
another had appeared to St. Lutgarde, telling her of her
approaching entrance into heaven. It is a beautiful thought,
this solicitude of the saints about their future companion, their
eagerness to advise and prepare her for her admission into their
joy! If we only realized how true this is in the case of us all!
If we only knew with what ardent and holy impatience the
charity of heaven's citizens longs to see us participating in their
endless beatitude.

Someone asked St. Lutgarde to explain how she saw these
saints. It seems that they did not appear individually before
her in imaginary visions, but that she saw them in an
intellectual vision of God Himself, or, to be more precise, in
the Word, in Christ. And here, perhaps, we find ourselves face
to face with the most difficult, the most subtle and the most
elevated of Lutgarde's visions.

This is how she described them. "From Christ Himself,"
she said, "from Christ who is the Saint of saints, and heaven's
Holy of Holies, I see a special spiritual splendor come forth,
and in this splendor I recognize perfectly whichever one of
the saints it is that appears to me."

"*De ipso Christo, sanctorum Sancto, quidam animae
illucens splendor egreditur. . . .*" There is much contained
in that play on words, "*sanctorum sancto.*" Christ is the Saint
of saints. He is Himself the sanctity of the saints. Their whole
merit and their glory is simply a share in His merit and His
glory, a participation in the inheritance of His divine Sonship,
and they are pleasing to the Father only in so far as the Father
sees His Son in them. He is, in a sense, the Holy of Holies
in heaven. He is the Head of the glorified Mystical Body, and,

22 *Vita,* 207 c.

therefore, its vital center, its life, the principle of all its being and activity.

Therefore we can see how, seeing the glorified Christ, St. Lutgarde was able to see all the other saints *in Him*. Not only that, but if we prayerfully meditate on this vision, we will soon come to find out that there is really no other way in which one *could* see the saints in heaven, especially in their present condition, without their risen bodies.

Finally, Thomas of Cantimpré concludes his account of these visions by saying that Lutgarde, mindful of the duty imposed upon her by Christ, did not omit to ask each one of the saints who thus appeared to her to offer thanks to God on her behalf, for all the favors He had given her in her life. Evidently, when Jesus had imposed this task upon His spouse, He had had in mind this special manner of making it easy for her.

Finally dawned a joyful day for Lutgarde, sad for her dear friends in this world: a day which Thomas of Cantimpré had prayed to be allowed to anticipate with his own death: a day which left him lamenting his lot, and declaring that he had been left an orphan. On June 9, a Saturday, the day before the second Sunday after Pentecost, which Thomas calls the "Octave of the Holy and undivided Trinity,"[23] St. Lutgarde entered upon the final stages of her sickness.

It soon became clear to all that the saint was dying. Just how many more days she had left was not clear. On the following Monday a lay brother of Afflighem saw her, and remarked that he wished his Father Abbot, a good friend of St. Lutgarde's as we have seen,[24] could be there.

"He will be here tomorrow," said the saint.

The lay brother, unwilling to contradict her, kept silent.

---

[23] . . . vigilia . . . octavarum Sanctae et individuae Trinitatis . . . (*Vita*, 207 f).

[24] This was Abbot John I, who ruled Afflighem from 1242 to 1261.

The very next day the abbot of Afflighem, on a journey, happened to pass within two miles of Aywières and, as he was on the road, he said to his companions:

"It is a long time since I last saw Mother Lutgarde. Let us turn aside and go over to Aywières."

When the Benedictine entered the saint's sickroom, she raised herself up in bed and greeted him with joy, saying:

"I am about to start for heaven, dear friend: and you are the best of all those I leave behind me."[25]

A day passed, then another. On the Thursday of that week — it would have been Corpus Christi, if that feast had been instituted — Lutgarde looked up and said to Sybil de Gages:

"Come and sit here close to my heart. For look, the monastery is all filled with the soldiers of the heavenly army: the souls of the blessed are here present with us, and among them are many, many of our sisters who have gone before us out of this world."

Yes, all her friends who had before come to summon and to advise her singly, had now gathered in a tremendous multitude. She could see the whole convent packed with them, as though they were jostling one another in the corridors, and the doorways, and in the cloister, waiting to catch up their new companion with a song of exultation, and begin their journey home into the realms of light.

With these words St. Lutgarde fell silent and remained rapt in spirit, her face shining with happiness for more than a day — the whole Friday that followed. Finally, on the Saturday, she returned to herself long enough to receive the Last Sacraments, and then, at last, took flight, peacefully and quietly to the kingdom of her Bridegroom with her friends, the glorious saints.

With the saints, we have said. But even the King of saints,

[25] *Vita*, 208 a.

it would seem, had come in person to escort her home. Thomas relates that at the moment of St. Lutgarde's passing, several of the most saintly nuns, in different parts of the convent, were suddenly filled with a mighty and overwhelming mystical joy which must have been caused, he thinks, by the very presence of Christ in the house.[26]

The holy Dominican closes the paragraph relating her death with a crescendo of Latin almost as impressive as the Christmas martyrology: "It was then the year twelve hundred and forty-six since the Incarnation of our Lord, in the month of June, on the sixteenth day before the calends of July, in the fourth indiction, in the sixty-fourth year of her life, the hour being about vespers, in the reign of our Lord Jesus Christ, to whom is all honor and glory, with the Father and the Holy Ghost, for ever and ever, Amen."[27]

It was the sixteenth of June, the same day of the month on which St. Margaret Mary was to have her famous vision of the Sacred Heart, in the year 1675.

[26] . . . et nimirum perfecte sentirent, quod cum immenso tripudio supernorum ipse praesentialiter nostrae salutis Princeps Jesus, animam illius ad delicias evocaverit paradisi (*Vita*, 208 b).

[27] *Vita, loc. cit.* The comparison to the martyrology applies to the Roman, rather than the Cistercian rite. The Cistercian martyrology for Christmas lacks the grandeur of the Roman, and is much shorter.

CHAPTER NINE

AFTER HER DEATH. MIRACLES. CULT

THE body of St. Lutgarde, like that of many other saints, preserved an extraordinary beauty and freshness even in death. She was not yet in the grave when God deigned to show by a miracle how pleased He was with the life of love and sacrifice she had led, and thus to give an indication that the faithful would find their petitions readily answered, if they had confidence in her intercession.

Among the nuns who were engaged, according to the Rule, in washing the body and preparing it for burial, there was one with a paralyzed hand. She happened to touch the body with that hand, and at that very instant its full use was restored to her, and the hand remained in perfect condition.

As Lutgarde's body lay exposed in the open bier in the choir of the convent church, and while the faithful were crowding to pray by the mortal remains of the saint—and not hesitating to despoil her of fragments of her clothing as relics—the nuns were discussing the problem of where to bury her, for it was manifest that she did not belong in the convent cemetery, like an ordinary nun.

The Abbot of Aulne, Father Immediate of the monastery, was on the scene, and as soon as the matter was placed before him he settled it in a word:

"Bury her in the church, of course!"

Where else indeed? It was fitting, as Thomas of Cantimpré points out, that her sisters and the faithful at large should be able to come and pray to God through her intercession, in the church where she had spent such long hours in intimate union with Christ, in anticipation of the heaven which she now enjoyed.

Besides, during the last days, one of the sisters had lamented the fact that St. Lutgarde was leaving them. But the saint had replied: "Come to my tomb: I will be as close to you there after my death as I am in my life."[1]

Thomas of Cantimpré managed to find, in this sentence, a kind of implicit prophecy that she would not be buried in the cemetery, but would indeed have a tomb worthy of being visited by pilgrims. And, after all, it was still not common to bury members of the Order in Cistercian churches, although, indeed, in the thirteenth century the practice was becoming more widespread, especially in the Low Countries.[2]

Even those who died in the odor of sanctity were seldom buried anywhere but in the common cemetery of the religious, and were only translated later to the cloister or the chapter room, and, perhaps after a second translation, to the church itself.[3]

In those days, the decrees of Urban VIII had not yet come into force, and although Alexander III had definitely reserved the right of formal canonization to the Holy See, local cults were still allowed to grow up everywhere, according to the devotion of the faithful, subject only to the surveillance of the bishops. That is why even after the practice of canonization by formal process was introduced, there were still

[1] *Vita,* 209 b.

[2] The Abbey of Villers was celebrated for the number of Cistercian "Blessed" buried and venerated in the abbey church, including Bl. Arnulph, the lay brother, Bl. Gobert of Aspremont, Bl. Godfrey the Sacristan, and the famous Augustinian nun, propagatress of the devotion to the Bl. Sacrament, Bl. Juliana of Mount Cornillon, whose last years were spent in the Cistercian convent of Salsinnes.

[3] Cf. M. Seraphin, O.C.S.O., *La Vénération des Saints (Cisterciens) dans l'Ordre., Collectanea,* Annus VI, p. 175 ff.

so many saints that were never formally canonized or whose cults were only officially recognized by the Holy See centuries later.

This was especially true, of course, of the saints of contemplative and enclosed Orders, which showed practically no interest in the canonizing of their members, and, in fact, even tended to discourage public cults in many cases as being a nuisance by destroying the peace and quiet of the community. St. Bruno, for instance, the founder of the Chartreuse, was never formally canonized. Neither were our own SS. Stephen Harding and Alberic, nor St. Gertrude the Great, who nevertheless is on the Calendar of the universal Church. The same applies to many another popular medieval saint, and St. Lutgarde herself, as we shall see, while being venerated with great fervor by the faithful for many centuries, did not receive official recognition from the Holy See until 1584.

However, her body had hardly been placed in the tomb when pilgrims began to come from all parts, and the custom sprang up of placing sprays of lilies on the stone slab that covered her relics, and which was fenced off with a wrought-iron railing. Lilies, it appears, had been her favorite flower.

From now on, we thread our way through a mass of curious details: for the veneration of saints, in the Middle Ages, was something in which imagination led men into expressions of devotion that were sometimes quaint and edifying, and at others eccentric and strange. Fortunately, St. Lutgarde's case is a comparatively simple one.

The modern reader will probably find that the devotion of Thomas of Cantimpré to his spiritual mother took a distinctly grisly turn when he began to plan, even before her death, on getting one of her hands cut off as a relic. That alone would be nothing very unusual.

However, after Thomas had asked the permission of the

Abbess to have St. Lutgarde's right hand cut off, the good
lady could not, as he bitterly complains, keep quiet about the
affair, and eventually news of it reached St. Lutgarde herself.

So one day when he came to visit her, the saint turned
a serious gaze upon him and said:

"Listen, my son. I understand that you are planning to cut
off one of my hands after I am dead. Why should you want
to do such a thing as that? What good will my hand be
to you?"

Thomas was very embarrassed, and began to blush, and
explained:

"I believe that your hand will be the occasion of much
good to myself, both spiritually and physically, if I obtain it,
as I intend."

Then Lutgarde smiled, and, raising up her right hand, she
laid the ring finger on the sill of the window through which
they were speaking, and said:

"You will have to be satisfied with this: because, after my
death, that is all you are going to get."

Emboldened by her cheerful tone, Thomas replied that
he would certainly not be satisfied with anything less than
a hand, or even her whole head. A fine way to be talking to
a nun, indeed! However, manners were different in those days.

Thomas was not able to be present at the saint's death,
but a couple of lay brothers who served the sisters of Aywières
went to the body, and were planning to cut off a hand, as a
relic, but somehow thought that would be too much, and
contended themselves with one finger and sixteen of her teeth.

When the good Dominican arrived on the scene he heard
about the harvest of relics, but did not know which finger
it was. So he said to himself: "So: they cut off one of your
fingers, Mother Lutgarde! Now we shall see whether you
really are a prophetess or not."

Sure enough, it turned out to be the ring finger of her

right hand. However, the Abbess, although she had previously
granted permission for the whole hand, now refused him even
the finger, and he did not get it until he returned a second
time to the attack, with the promise that he would write
the saint's biography.[4]

As a theologian, however, he seems to have felt that his
avidity for relics needed some justification, so he cited the
case of St. Nathaly, who cut off the arm of her husband St.
Adrian after his martyrdom, as well as Jacques de Vitry who
had appropriated a finger of Bl. Mary of Oignies, right after
her death, and had worn it around his neck, until he finally
made a present of it to Pope Gregory IX, to help him in
a particular interior trial.

The nuns of Aywières were not as bold as the Dominican
Friar. They did not proceed with the dismembering of their
sister's body, but they did descend upon all that was left of
the objects that had been given her for her use in the convent,
and her clothes and everything else were torn up and distributed as relics.

Her veil cured one of the nuns of a disease of the throat,
and another of severe headaches. A noble matron of the
district, laboring grievously in a hard childbirth, was quickly
delivered when a horsehair cord, which St. Lutgarde had used
as an instrument of penance, was placed about her waist.

Other relics cured swollen thumbs and hands, and various
wounds and ills, but the number of miracles went on increasing long after the time when Thomas finished his
short biography.

Meanwhile, he tells us that one of his own relatives — also
a nun — was cured of chronic headaches and of some kind
of allergy to lilies on a visit to St. Lutgarde's tomb. Indeed, he
says, she even detested the very sight of a lily, and on that

[4] *Vita,* 208 e.

account, she could hardly be persuaded to enter the church, much less go near the tomb. When the first faint breath of lilies reached her in the doorway she stopped dead, and refused to take another step. However, perceiving that the usual ill-effects did not begin to make themselves felt, she advanced cautiously into the building, and finally went right up to the tomb and smelled the lilies outright. From then on she was cured both of her headaches and of her allergy.

Of course, a cure like this might very well have been no cure at all. There are plenty of headaches and allergies that have no organic cause whatever, and are rooted in some neurotic twist in the patient's make-up.

However, here is one that is not so easy to explain away as "purely psychological," although the same nun was the subject of the cure. Having lost her fear of lilies, and having become an ardent client of the saint, this sister used to pay frequent visits to the tomb at all hours of the day and night. Once, in the darkness of the night, she went there to pray, and prostrated on the floor before the railing, as was apparently her custom. Unfortunately, in the darkness, she got too close to the iron work, and actually drove her head against one of the protruding iron spikes, which plunged into her eye, and practically gouged the eye out of its socket. This time there was no question of neurosis or imagination. The pain was intolerable, and she had to hold her eye with her hand to prevent it falling from the socket. She had enough strength and presence of mind to pray to St. Lutgarde, and complain of the injury she had received when she had come to pray for favors. Then she groped her way out of the church and headed for the infirmary. And yet, says Thomas, within an hour her injury was completely cured.[5]

Meanwhile St. Lutgarde did not content herself with

[5] *Vita,* 209 f.

merely answering prayers. Soon after the burial of the saint, her friend Elizabeth de Wans was at prayer, when Lutgarde appeared before her in great glory.

The first thing Elizabeth asked her was if she had had to spend any time in purgatory — a very practical, and, at the same time, very feminine question.

"No," replied St. Lutgarde, "not only did I pass directly to heaven, without going through purgatory, but on my way past the place of trial, I felt sorrow for the poor souls, and blessed them, and, by the mercy of God, many of them were set free, and accompanied me to paradise."

As Elizabeth was still pondering on these words, she saw the saint turn toward a young nun, Sister Matilda, and say: "Come with me."

Apparently Elizabeth was the only one who saw and heard this: but she took it at once to mean that the saint was calling the young sister to heaven.

"Oh," cried Elizabeth, "please let me come with you too, Mother!"

"You cannot follow me yet," said St. Lutgarde, "but in due time you will do so: you are my daughter, and you will come and join me, your mother."[6]

Within nine days, Sister Matilda died. We do not know exactly when Bl. Elizabeth went to heaven: but the date tentatively assigned for her death was some four years later, in 1250.[7]

Another, much more interesting vision, and one with a certain amount of mystery about it, occurred when the convent was visited by the plague. This affliction fell upon Aywières soon after the saint's death, and struck the community with such devastating effect that within a short space fourteen of the most fervent and valuable sisters

---

[6] *Vita*, 209 c.
[7] *Actes . . . concernant le Menologe Cistercian*, 1937, p. 49.

died. Thomas himself was present when two of the nuns, who were sisters according to the flesh as well as sisters in religion, died within a few minutes of each other, and were buried in the same tomb, after he had sung Mass over them.

In the midst of this frightful disaster the Sisters remembered that St. Lutgarde had reproved those who said the Office without sufficient care and reverence in the infirmary chapel, and had warned them that if they did not improve, the whole convent would have to pay for their neglect. At once the offenders began to apply themselves with renewed zeal to the recitation of the hours, and no sooner had they mended their ways than the plague ceased.

Now while the plague was in progress, one of the nuns of Aywières had a vision, or, more probably a dream, in which she saw men attacking the convent church, breaking into it and invading it in large numbers so that no one could keep them out, until St. Lutgarde rose from her tomb and drove them all before her, out the doors, until she had cleared the sacred precincts of all defilers.

Thomas of Cantimpré, writing two years after the event, thought this had something to do with the ending of the plague. But we may be bold enough to suggest another explanation.

The subsequent history of the convent of Aywières has much in it that bears out this dream of a thirteenth-century nun. For two hundred years after the death of St. Lutgarde, although the regularity of the community gradually and slowly declined and became relaxed, nevertheless the course of events was smooth enough. The biggest trial the convent had to suffer was the burden of taxes in the fourteenth century, imposed by secular princes to wage their endless wars.

But when the weak, top-heavy structure of medieval culture finally collapsed, because of the tepidity of so many of the faithful, and when the religious wars began to devastate the face of Europe, Aywières had to suffer indeed.

An eyewitness account, probably by a Cistercian nun or monk, tells of what took place in 1567 and 1568.[8]

On the night of March 18, 1567, the dream of the thirteenth-century nun was really fulfilled. The community at Aywières was sleeping in the dormitory. A troop of sixty soldiers arrived, scaled the walls, and were swarming through the cloisters before anyone was aware of their arrival. The nuns were awakened by the crash of a huge battering ram against the locked, iron-banded door of the dormitory. The crashing wood, the thunder of feet upon the stairs, the cries and curses of the men terrified the nuns. They rushed down the stairway at the other end of the dormitory and into the church, and flung themselves down in prayer before the altar of the Blessed Virgin.

However, the world had need of victims – and there were several hundred years of growing immorality and avarice, and infidelity to be atoned for. After about an hour's work, the soldiers finally succeeded in breaking down the dormitory door, and charged through the room and down into the church. The nuns had huddled together in a group with their arms locked together, and refused to be separated, but the bloodthirsty cutthroats battered them with their fists, or cut their arms savagely with their daggers, and forced them apart, shouting their demands that the chalices and other precious objects be handed over to them, while at the same time claiming payment of ransom for some prelate whom they held prisoner.

---

[8] *Analectes pour servir à l'histoire ecclésiastique de Belgique*, t. vi (1869), 304 ff. Quoted in Canivez, *L'Ordre de Citeaux en Belgique*, p. 175. The narration is entitled: "Mémoire de ce qui est arrivé à l'abbaye d' Aywières pendant les guerres des ans 1567, 1568."

The main objective of the marauders was money, plate, and valuables: but they did not hesitate to beat and kick the nuns, and drag them around cruelly until they were covered with blood. Some of them were nearly killed. This lasted the whole night long. The chronicler does not tell us what else may have happened to the unfortunate sisters: but by three o'clock in the morning the soldiers were gone, taking with them anything of any value that was in the monastery.

It must be emphasized that these men were not necessarily Protestants. Belgium was, at that time, overrun with French, Spanish, and other troops, and all of them were equally unprincipled. The only thing that might be said was that with men from Catholic countries, the chief interest was plunder, while the Protestants, although no less interested in the silver and gold and fine linen and plate which the convents and monasteries possessed, were also intent upon killing the nuns, desecrating sanctuaries, destroying statues, and so on. The Catholics did not have this formal hatred of their own religion, but, apart from that, a convent was hardly safer in the hands of the French or Spanish than when it was at the mercy of the Gueux. The reason for this was that the men who composed the armies on both sides were all equally without religion. Their leaders may have had certain external principles, but the rank and file of those armies was made up of unlettered, brutalized savages, men who had lost their humanity and become wolves and bears, who had long ago forgotten the name of God except to blaspheme it, and who, perhaps, had never received any sacrament beyond baptism.

After that the nuns had to construct special hiding places for every useful implement, from the choir books to the cooking pots and pans. Nothing was safe, and they suffered from these sporadic raids from time to time, for ten years. Finally, in 1579, they were driven out altogether, and were forced to wander about from place to place for twelve years, while

Aywières became a robbers' hide-out, and was finally burned
to the ground.

So much for the sufferings of the community! But they had
not lost the relics of St. Lutgarde, and in 1600 the convent
rosc again from its ruins, in newness and simplicity, and the
peaceful life of religion began there once again for another
two hundred years.

However, before those dark days of the sixteenth century,
Aywières and St. Lutgarde's tomb had long been a center of
pilgrimage, and the cult revived in full force in the seventeenth century, especially since it was at last officially recognized by Rome, in the very blackest period of the convent's
crisis, in 1584, when the buildings were left desolate and the
church was a den of thieves.

In that year Lutgarde was inscribed in the Roman Martyrology, and, probably on the return of the nuns, her relics
were elevated and placed under an altar dedicated to her. The
date of this elevation is not certain, but we find the fact
recorded in the *Gazophylacium Belgicum* of Rayssius, written
in 1628.[9]

Before that, in 1565, Margaret of Parma, Governess of the
Low Countries, had sent some relics of St. Lutgarde to King
Henry of Portugal, and therefore it is probable that in the
seventeenth century the distribution of her relics was under
episcopal control. The same relics that had been sent to the
King of Portugal were afterward treasured at the Abbey of
the Holy Saviour, at Antwerp.

Meanwhile, the faithful had continued to place their lilies
on St. Lutgarde's tomb, and expectant mothers used to put
her girdle about their waists for a safe delivery, or sit in the
choir stall she had once used. That does not necessarily mean
that they went into the nuns' choir to do so — although almost

9 Quoted in Jonquet, *op. cit.*, p. 216.

anything is possible in the state of irregularity to which the Cistercian Order had descended by that time. The old stall she had occupied as prioress of St. Catherine's was long preserved in a Benedictine monastery at Milen, and today it may still be seen in a convent of Bernardine nuns, an offshoot of the Cistercian family, at Colen. It is probably this stall that attracted pilgrims in the old days, and not one at Aywières.

In 1741 the Bishop of Namur declared that he desired to encourage and increase the devotion of the faithful to St. Lutgarde, and granted indulgences to all who venerated her image and her relics. His rescript was confirmed by his successors in 1773 and 1783.

Although the Abbey of Aywières was finally destroyed in the French revolution, the relics of St. Lutgarde were saved, and the nuns took them along in their wanderings from place to place, from castle to castle, wherever anyone would give them shelter for a while. The year 1804 found the last remaining nuns keeping their mitigated Rule near the village of Ittré, the parish Church of which finally fell heir to the relics of St. Lutgarde and Bl. Sybil de Gages. The last abbess of Aywières, seeing that there was no further hope of ever rebuilding the convent, turned the relics over to that parish in 1819. The elaborate reliquaries enclosing the various major relics of the saint date from the seventeenth century, and testify to the vigor of the cult in her honor, after the return of the nuns to their renovated convent following the wars of religion.

But the veneration of the faithful for St. Lutgarde did not die out with the destruction of Aywières. The nineteenth century saw a renewal of all the indulgences and their confirmation by the Holy See. In 1838, an indult of the Sacred Congregation of Rites placed her among the saints venerated in the Archdiocese of Mechlin, with a feast on the sixteenth of June. In 1872, the archbishop of that same see attached a forty days' indulgence to a prayer to St. Lutgarde. Her feast is also celebrated in the diocese of Namur.

In the ancient Cistercian calendar there were practically no feasts of saints of our Order, besides Sts. Bernard, Peter of Tarentaise, and William of Bourges. Even in the *Menology* of Henriquez, printed at Antwerp in 1630, we find an enthusiastic eulogy of St. Lutgarde, but no mention of a feast in her honor in the Order. No doubt the work of Henriquez and Manrique and other Cistercian chroniclers of the seventeenth century did much to draw attention to the saints of the Order, and when, under the Abbot General, Claude Vaussin, the General Chapter of 1651 undertook a complete reform of the Cistercian Breviary and other liturgical books, many feasts of Cistercian saints appeared in the revised version. Thus, although we lost most of our own ancient liturgy, in the "corrections" that the fathers of that time considered so necessary, we did gain many feasts of our own saints. There was St. Stephen Harding, for instance, with a feast of two Masses on April 17. Then SS. Francha, Sacerdos, Robert of Newminster, Hedwig, and Galgan had feasts of three lessons. Our own St. Lutgarde had a feast of twelve lessons, equivalent to the rite of "duplex" or double, which she still enjoys in the dioceses of Mechlin and Namur. Her Office, including the Collect, was taken entirely from the Common of Virgins except for the proper lessons of the second nocturn, giving a brief résumé of her life, following Thomas of Cantimpré.

In the course of various Breviary reforms since that day, St. Lutgarde has not fared so well as some of our other saints. St. Stephen Harding now has his rightful position in our sanctoral cycle with a feast of Sermon major, with octave, and many new saints have been introduced into the Calendar with feasts or commemorations. Among those whose rank has been reduced is St. Lutgarde, who has fallen to a feast of three lessons, equivalent to the Roman "semiduplex." We still sing her name in our litany of the saints.

Another series of changes in the Cistercian Breviary is at present being planned, and we may hope that St. Lutgarde will not be forgotten.

For, after all, Cistercians of our day have much to gain by the contemplation of that life of sacrifice and of love. The story of St. Lutgarde will amply repay our meditation, whether we be monks, or nuns, or priests, or seminarians, or married people, or Christians in the world.

It is a lesson that the Sacred Heart ardently desires us to learn. Whoever we are, whatever may be our state of life, we are called to the glory and freedom of the sons of God. Our vocation is union with Christ. We are coheirs with Him of His own divine glory. We share His divine Sonship.

If Jesus has raised up saints like Lutgarde in the Church, it has always been with one end in view: to remind men of their glorious vocation and to inspire them with courage and love to forsake the shadow of worldly felicity and to embrace the Cross, in order to follow Him to true peace and true joy of heart.

St. Lutgarde is there, wounded with the wounds of Christ's love, sharing in His Passion, for our sakes, that we may learn, from her, to despise our own wills, renounce that mean and petty preoccupation with ourselves which freezes and contracts the heart, and keeps us living, all our days, in the shadows of worry, and jealousy, and fear. She is there, with her own bleeding heart, to inspire us to take up arms against our selfishness, and storm heaven with love and abnegation.

BIBLIOGRAPHY

Aelredi, S., abbatis Rievallensis, *Opera*, Migne, *P.L.*

Acta Sanctorum, Vol. 24 (June, ii) (Paris, 1867), p. 187 ff.

Actes de la commission de Liturgie concernant le Menologe Cistercien (Westmalle, 1937).

Bernardi, S., *Opera Omnia*, ed. Mabillon.

Breviarium Cisterciense (old rite) (Salamanca, 1595).

Breviarium Cisterciense juxta Romanum (Paris, 1657).

Cantimpré, Thomas of, O.P., *Vita Lutgardis*, see *Acta Sanctorum*.

Canivez, Dom J. M., O.C.R., *Statuta Capituli Generalis ordinis Cisterciensis*.

—— *L'Ordre de Citeaux en Belgique* (Scourmont, 1926).

Collectanea O.C.R. (periodical) (Westmalle: 1932 ff.).

Duns Scoti, J., *Opera* (Paris: Vives, 1893).

John of the Cross, St., *The Ascent of Mount Carmel*.

—— *The Dark Night of the Soul*.

—— *The Living Flame of Love* (in the French versions of Canon Hoornaert).

Jonquet, P., Obl. de Marie Immaculée, *Ste Lutgarde, la Marguerite Marie Belge* (Bruxelles, 1907).

Missale Cisterciense (old rite).

Mourret Thompson, *History of the Church*.

Nimal, P. H., C.SS.R., *Les Grandes Saintes du Pays de Liége* (Liége, 1898). (French trans. of Thos. of Cantimpré, p. 178 ff.)

—— *Fleurs Cisterciennes* (Liége, 1898).

Plogaerts, Abbé Th., *Histoire de l'Abbaye d' Aywières* (Bruxelles, 1925).

Poulain, A., *The Graces of Interior Prayer* (London).

Teresa of Avila, St., *The Interior Castle,* trans. by the Benedictine nuns of Stanbrook (London: Thos. Baker, 1930).

Thomae Aquinatis, St., *Opera Omnia* (Paris: Vives).